# Math Skills

## Grade 2

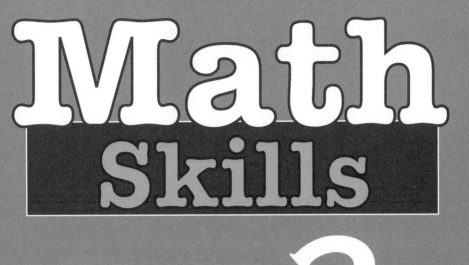

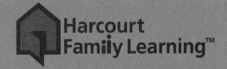

**Harcourt Family Learning™**

© 2004 by Flash Kids
Adapted from *Steck-Vaughn Working with Numbers, Level B*
© 2001 by Harcourt Achieve
Licensed under special arrangement with Harcourt Achieve.

Illustrator: Ed Shems

ISBN: 978-1-4114-0107-5

Please submit all inquiries to FlashKids@bn.com

Printed and bound in China

**Flash Kids**
A Division of Barnes & Noble
122 Fifth Avenue
New York, NY 10011

## Dear Parent,

You've already taken the first step toward your child's success by purchasing this book and making time to work with your child. Using *Math Skills* as a learning tool will make that time effective. This book contains fun illustrations and activities to keep your young learner entertained. In addition, *Math Skills* includes materials required by both state and national standards. If your child is learning it in school, this book covers it.

Starting with basics like place value and counting, followed by addition and subtraction with and without regrouping, your child will learn all the facts necessary to understanding second-grade math. In this book you'll also find sections on money, time, geometry and measurement. Throughout each unit, your child will be given ample opportunity to estimate, compare, find patterns, and use logic. Exercises like these help your child develop important thinking and problem-solving skills. These areas of knowledge are the foundation upon which your child will build more complex math skills.

One of the most difficult things about math is the potential frustration it poses for some young learners. *Math Skills* counteracts this problem by providing examples on almost every page. The harder topics are covered from many different angles, to ensure that your child can move forward snag-free, without giving up. In addition, the answer key at the back of the book can act as a reference for you and your child.

As you and your child work through the book, try to show your child how to apply new skills to everyday situations. For example, have your child estimate how many dozen eggs will be needed to make breakfast for the family for a week, or how much fencing will be needed to enclose your garden. As your child draws connections between concepts presented separately in this workbook, he or she learns to reason mathematically, an ability critical for success through future years of math instruction.

Also, consider how you can turn the following activities into fun math exercises for you and your child to do together:

- Determining the proper number of coins needed to buy different items at the grocery store;

- Calculating how much change will be given after a purchase;

- Estimating how much time is left before the next planned activity of the day;

- Making graphs to organize information, such as household chores or school progress;

- Using an inch ruler to chart the growth progress of a houseplant;

- Measuring ingredients for a recipe;

- Identifying symmetrical or congruent shapes in your home or around your neighborhood.

Use your imagination. With help from you and this workbook, your child is well on the way to math success!

# Table of Contents

## unit 1

## unit 2

## unit 3

# unit 4

# unit 5

# unit 6

# unit 7

## Counting to 50

Draw lines to match numbers and groups.

**27**

**44**

**19**

**35**

# Counting to 50
Write the missing numbers.

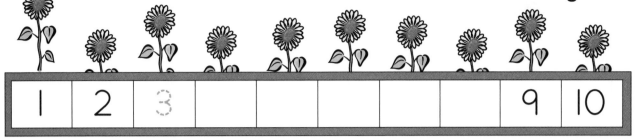

| 1 | 2 | 3 | | | | | | 9 | 10 |

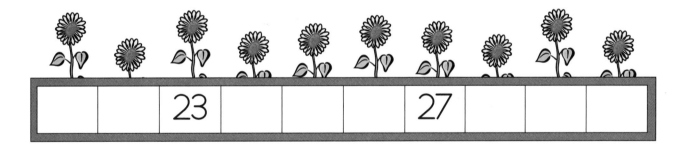

| 11 | | | | | 16 | | 18 | | |

| | | 23 | | | | 27 | | | |

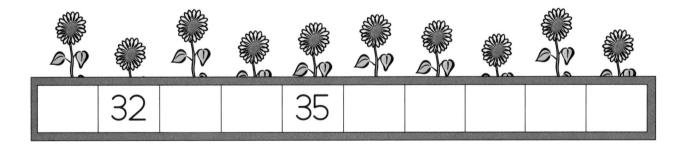

| | 32 | | | 35 | | | | | |

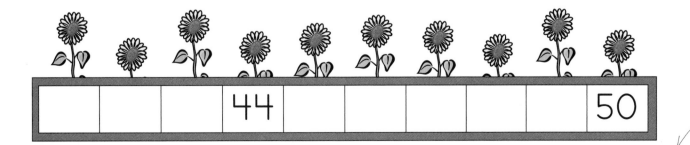

| | | 44 | | | | | | | 50 |

7

# Counting to 100

Write the missing numbers.

| | | | | | | | | | |
|---|---|---|---|---|---|---|---|---|---|
| 1 | 2 | 3 | | | | | | | |
| 11 | | | | 15 | | | | | |
| 21 | | | | | | | | | |
| | 32 | | | | | | 38 | | |
| | | | | 45 | | | | | |
| | 52 | | | | | | | | 60 |
| | | | 64 | | | | | | |
| | | | | | 76 | | | | 80 |
| | | | | | | 87 | | | |
| | | 93 | | | | | | | 100 |

Write the missing numbers in each row.

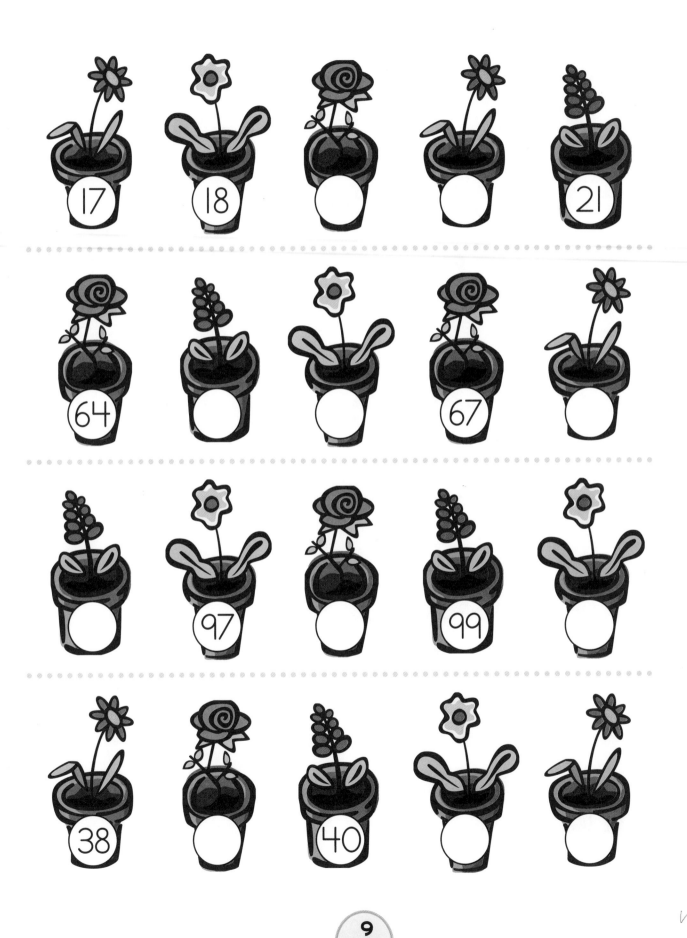

Row 1: 17, 18, ___, ___, 21

Row 2: 64, ___, ___, 67, ___

Row 3: ___, 97, ___, 99, ___

Row 4: 38, ___, 40, ___, ___

# Tens and Ones

Circle groups of ten. Write how many tens and ones.

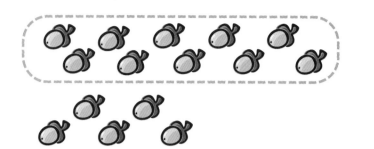

| Tens | Ones |
|------|------|
| 1    | 5    |

| Tens | Ones |
|------|------|
|      |      |

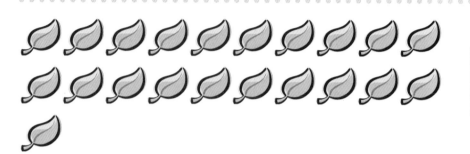

| Tens | Ones |
|------|------|
|      |      |

| Tens | Ones |
|------|------|
|      |      |

Write how many tens and ones. Then write the numbers.

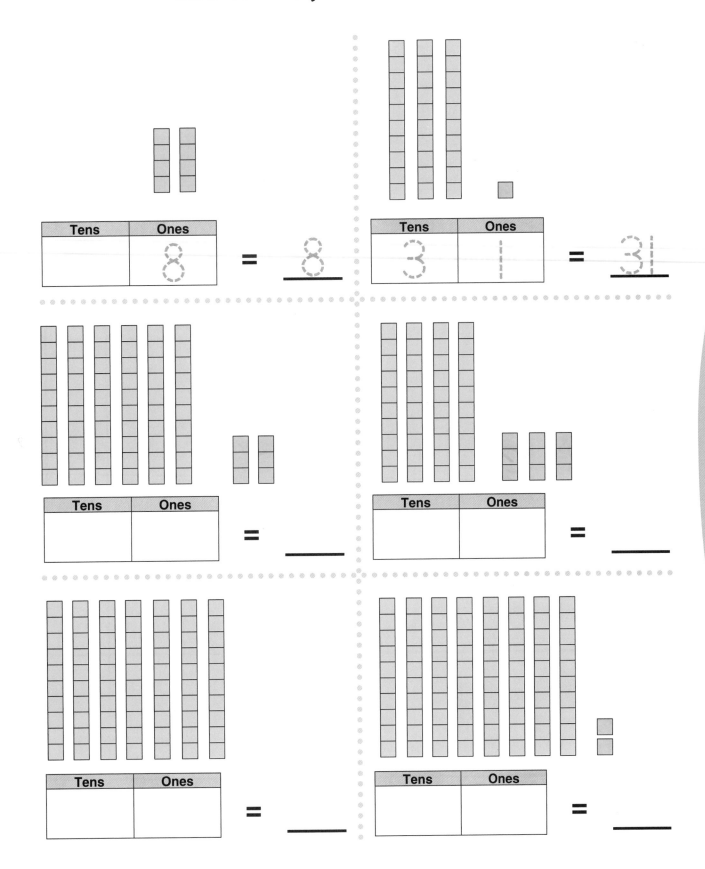

| Tens | Ones |
|------|------|
|      | 8    |

= 8

| Tens | Ones |
|------|------|
| 3    | 1    |

= 31

| Tens | Ones |
|------|------|
|      |      |

= ___

| Tens | Ones |
|------|------|
|      |      |

= ___

| Tens | Ones |
|------|------|
|      |      |

= ___

| Tens | Ones |
|------|------|
|      |      |

= ___

# Hundreds, Tens, and Ones

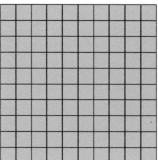

## Write how many hundreds, tens, and ones.

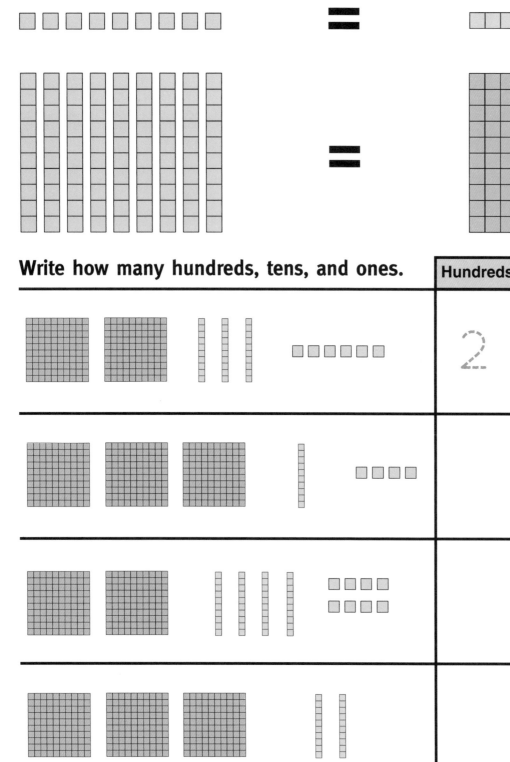

| Hundreds | Tens | Ones |
|----------|------|------|
| 2 | 3 | 6 |
| | | |
| | | |
| | | |
| | | |

# Hundreds, Tens, and Ones

Write how many hundreds, tens, and ones. Then write the numbers.

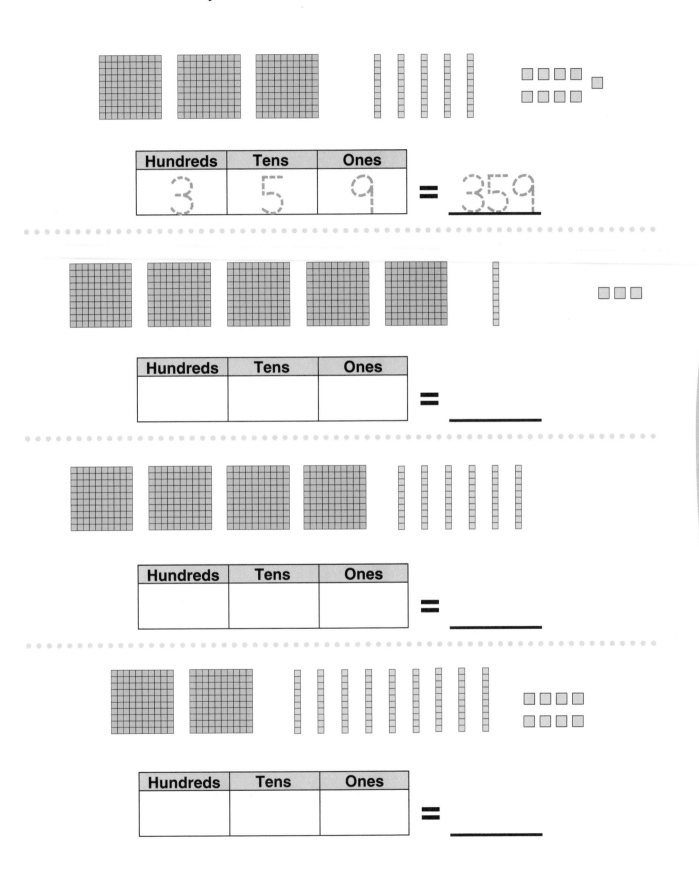

| Hundreds | Tens | Ones |
|----------|------|------|
| 3 | 5 | 9 |

= 359

| Hundreds | Tens | Ones |
|----------|------|------|
|  |  |  |

= _____

| Hundreds | Tens | Ones |
|----------|------|------|
|  |  |  |

= _____

| Hundreds | Tens | Ones |
|----------|------|------|
|  |  |  |

= _____

# Counting to 150

Write the missing numbers in each row.

Row 1: 139, 140, ___, 142, ___

Row 2: 98, ___, ___, ___, 102

Row 3: 116, ___, 118, ___, ___

Row 4: ___, ___, 148, 149, ___

**Write the missing numbers.**

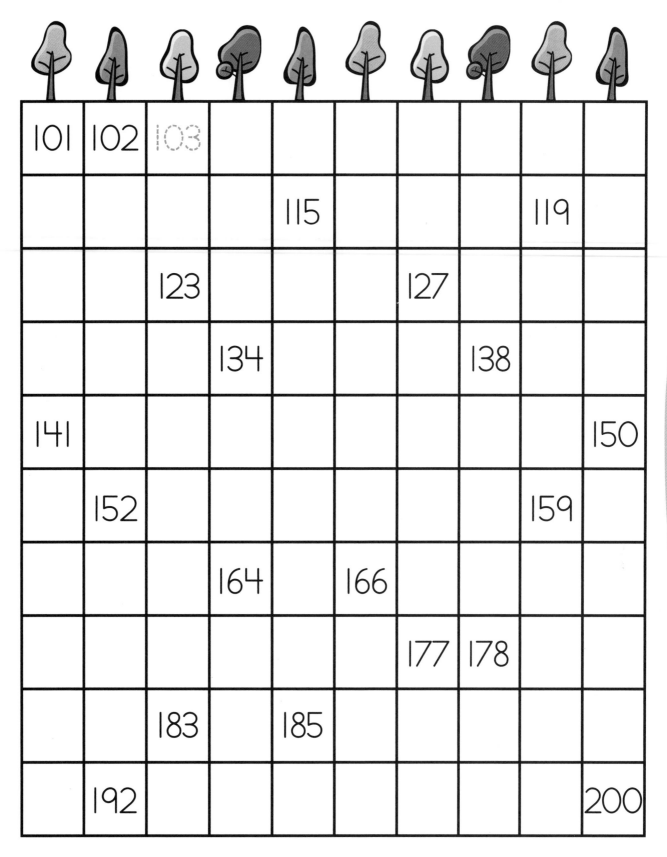

| | | | | | | | | | |
|---|---|---|---|---|---|---|---|---|---|
| 101 | 102 | 103 | | | | | | | |
| | | | | 115 | | | | 119 | |
| | | 123 | | | | 127 | | | |
| | | | 134 | | | | 138 | | |
| 141 | | | | | | | | | 150 |
| | 152 | | | | | | | 159 | |
| | | | 164 | | 166 | | | | |
| | | | | | | 177 | 178 | | |
| | | 183 | | 185 | | | | | |
| | 192 | | | | | | | | 200 |

# Make a Model

Match each number to its model.

**136**

**18**

**205**

**452**

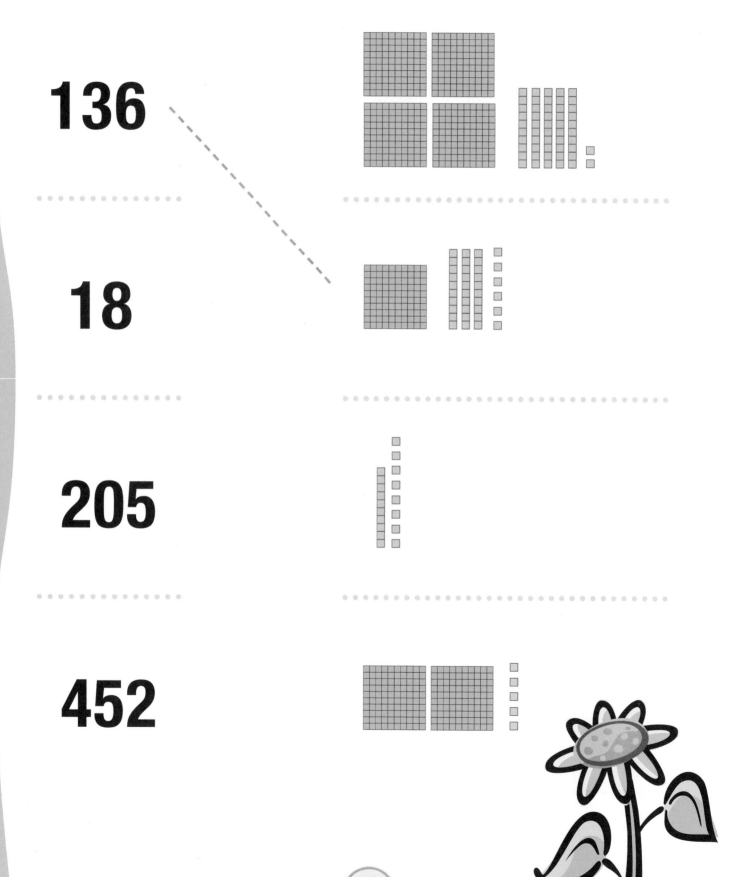

Count and compare. Write < or > in each box.

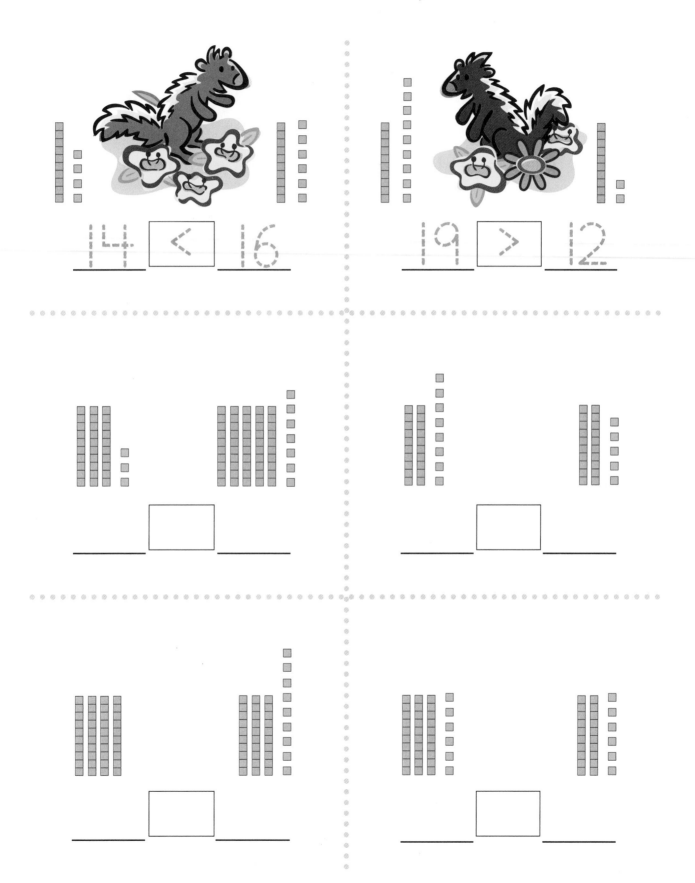

14 < 16

19 > 12

# Ordering Numbers

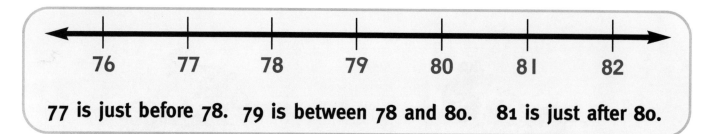

76   77   78   79   80   81   82

77 is just before 78.   79 is between 78 and 80.   81 is just after 80.

**Write the number that is just before, just after, or between.**

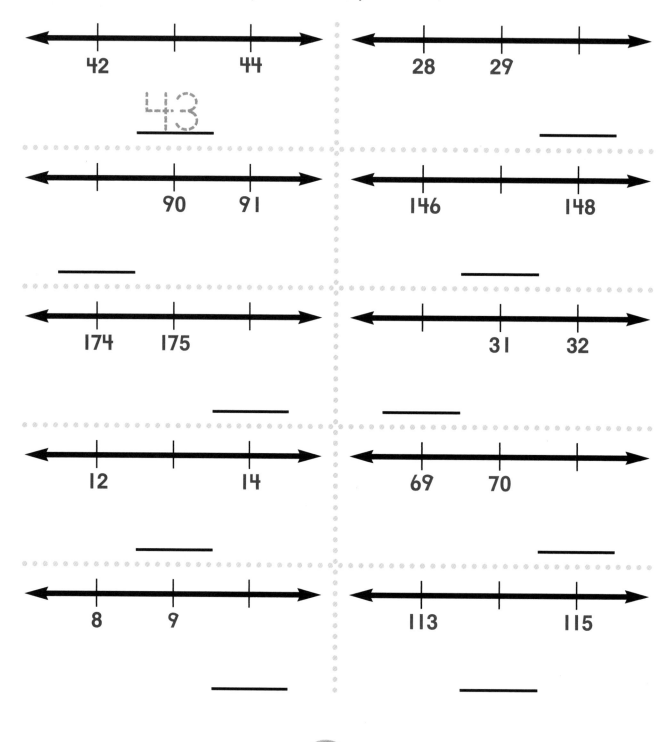

42 ___ 44
43

28  29 ___

___ 90  91

146 ___ 148

___ 174  175

___ 31  32

12 ___ 14

69  70 ___

8  9 ___

113 ___ 115

# Ordinal Numbers to Tenth

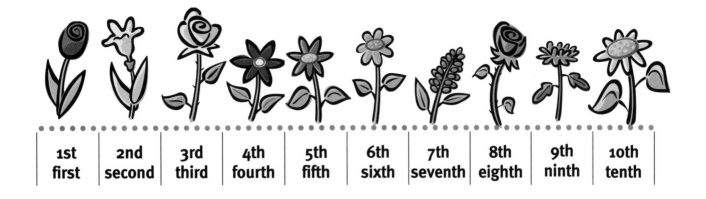

| 1st | 2nd | 3rd | 4th | 5th | 6th | 7th | 8th | 9th | 10th |
|------|--------|-------|--------|-------|-------|---------|--------|-------|-------|
| first | second | third | fourth | fifth | sixth | seventh | eighth | ninth | tenth |

**Write the position of each flower.**

seventh  
7th

fourth  
4th

# Ordinal Numbers to Twentieth

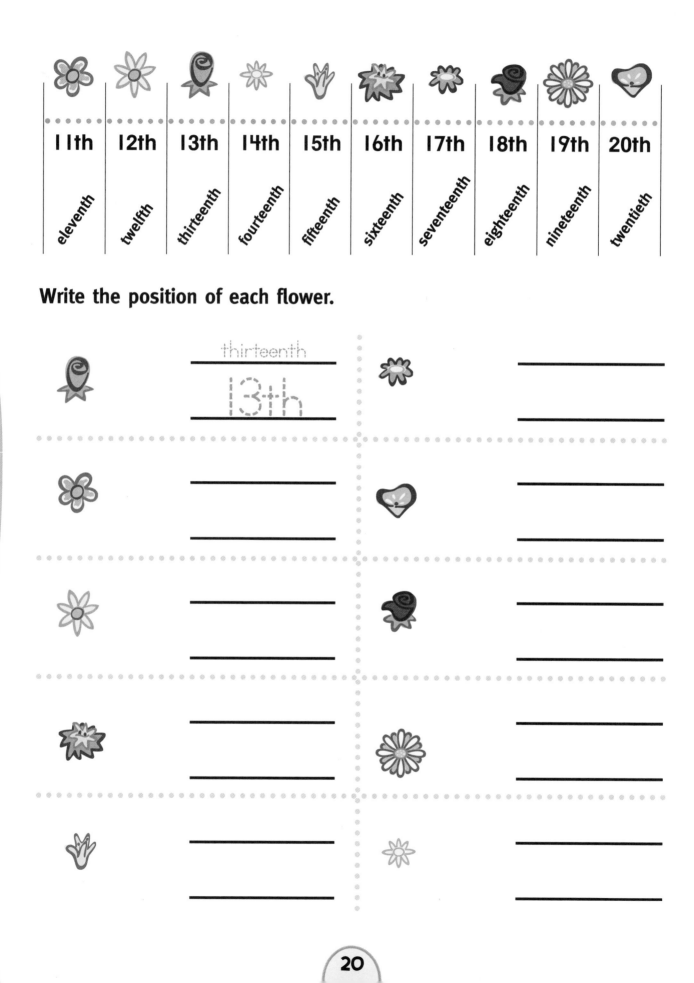

| 11th | 12th | 13th | 14th | 15th | 16th | 17th | 18th | 19th | 20th |
|------|------|------|------|------|------|------|------|------|------|
| eleventh | twelfth | thirteenth | fourteenth | fifteenth | sixteenth | seventeenth | eighteenth | nineteenth | twentieth |

**Write the position of each flower.**

thirteenth

13th

# Skip Counting by Fives and Tens

Skip count by fives or tens. Write the numbers.

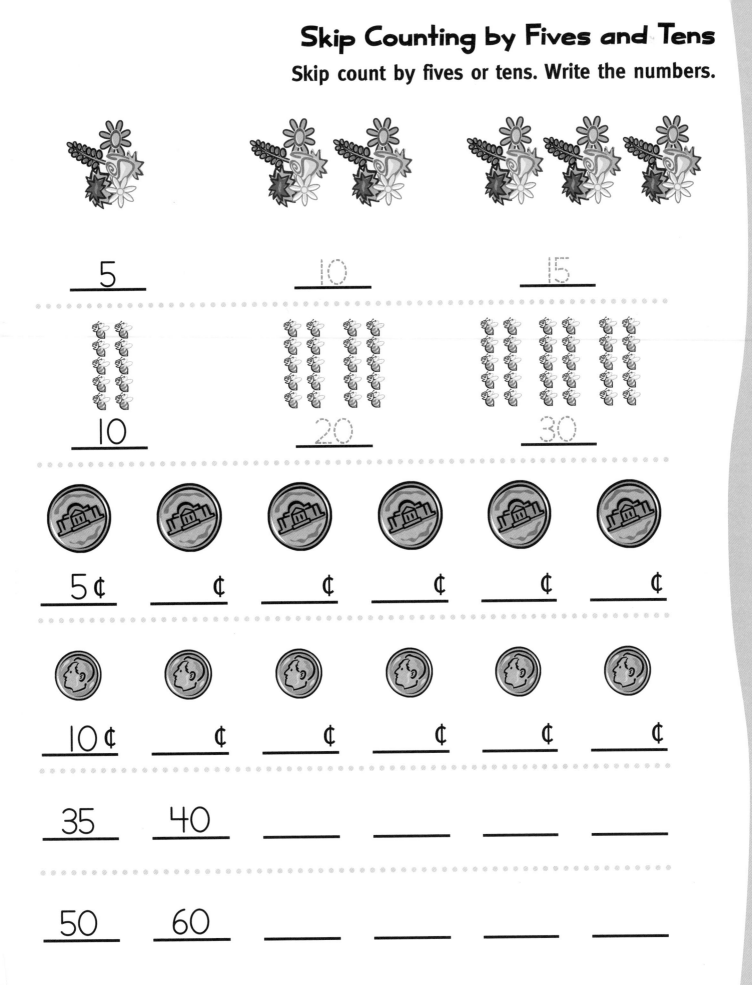

5      10      15

10      20      30

5¢    ___¢    ___¢    ___¢    ___¢    ___¢

10¢   ___¢    ___¢    ___¢    ___¢    ___¢

35    40    ___    ___    ___    ___

50    60    ___    ___    ___    ___

# Skip Counting by Twos

Skip count by twos. Write the numbers.

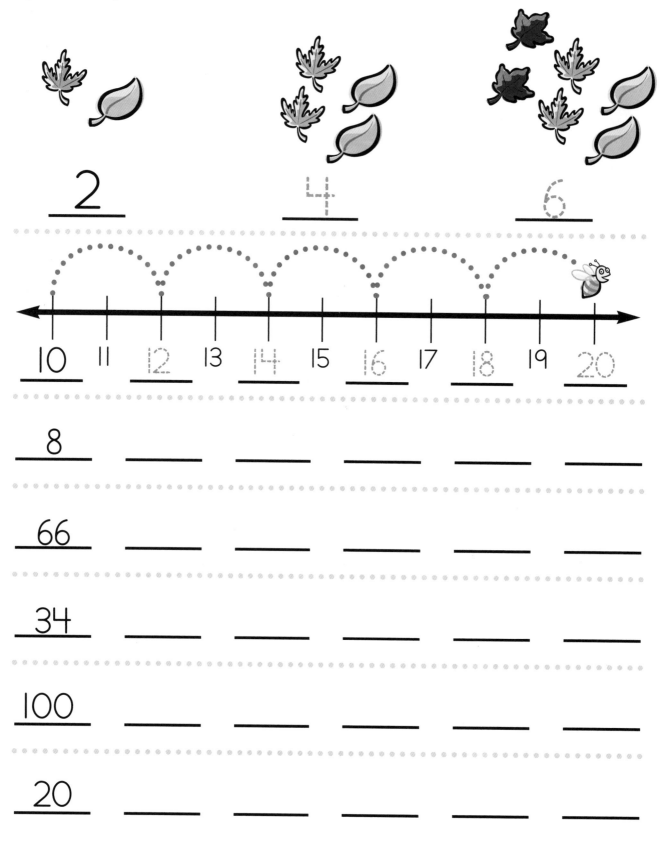

2  4  6

10 11 12 13 14 15 16 17 18 19 20

8 ___ ___ ___ ___ ___

66 ___ ___ ___ ___ ___

34 ___ ___ ___ ___ ___

100 ___ ___ ___ ___ ___

20 ___ ___ ___ ___ ___

# Even and Odd Numbers

Circle groups of 2. Then circle *even* or *odd*.

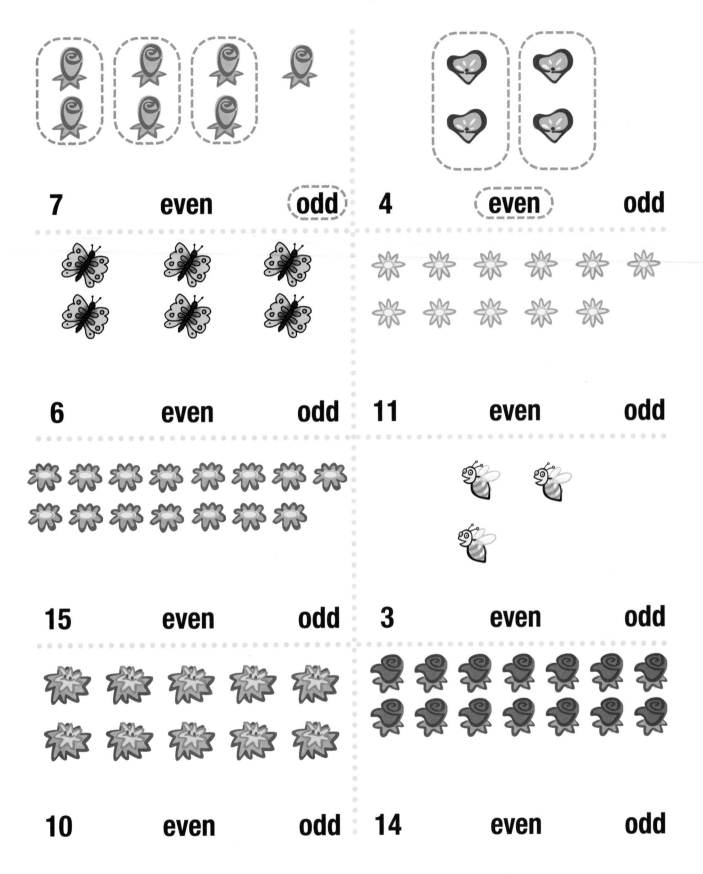

**7**     even     (odd)     **4**     (even)     odd

**6**     even     odd     **11**     even     odd

**15**     even     odd     **3**     even     odd

**10**     even     odd     **14**     even     odd

# Find a Pattern

Skip count by twos. Circle those numbers.
Skip count by fives. Color those boxes blue.

| 1 | 2 | 3 | 4 | 5 | 6 | 7 | 8 | 9 | 10 |
|---|---|---|---|---|---|---|---|---|----|
| 11 | 12 | 13 | 14 | 15 | 16 | 17 | 18 | 19 | 20 |
| 21 | 22 | 23 | 24 | 25 | 26 | 27 | 28 | 29 | 30 |
| 31 | 32 | 33 | 34 | 35 | 36 | 37 | 38 | 39 | 40 |
| 41 | 42 | 43 | 44 | 45 | 46 | 47 | 48 | 49 | 50 |
| 51 | 52 | 53 | 54 | 55 | 56 | 57 | 58 | 59 | 60 |
| 61 | 62 | 63 | 64 | 65 | 66 | 67 | 68 | 69 | 70 |
| 71 | 72 | 73 | 74 | 75 | 76 | 77 | 78 | 79 | 80 |
| 81 | 82 | 83 | 84 | 85 | 86 | 87 | 88 | 89 | 90 |
| 91 | 92 | 93 | 94 | 95 | 96 | 97 | 98 | 99 | 100 |

# Find a Pattern

Write the missing numbers in each row.

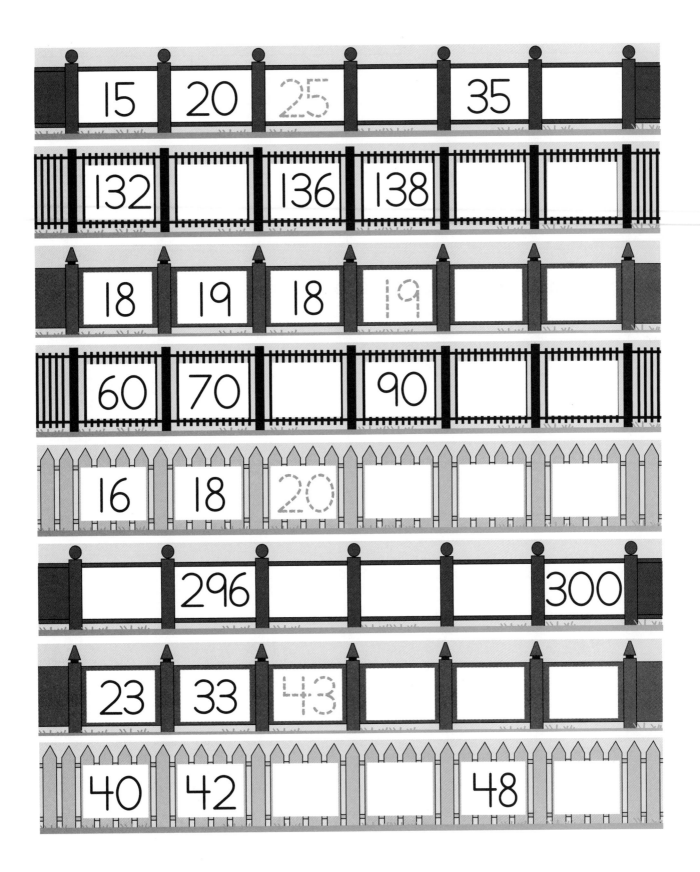

Row 1: 15, 20, 25, ___, 35, ___

Row 2: 132, ___, 136, 138, ___, ___

Row 3: 18, 19, 18, 19, ___, ___

Row 4: 60, 70, ___, 90, ___, ___

Row 5: 16, 18, 20, ___, ___, ___

Row 6: ___, 296, ___, ___, ___, 300

Row 7: 23, 33, 43, ___, ___, ___

Row 8: 40, 42, ___, ___, 48, ___

25

**Write the missing numbers in each row.**

| 36 | | | 39 | | | |
|----|----|----|----|----|----|----|

| 71 | | | | 76 | | |
|----|----|----|----|----|----|----|

| 113 | | | 117 | | | |
|-----|----|----|-----|----|----|----|

| 185 | | | | | | 192 |
|-----|----|----|----|----|----|-----|

**Count and compare. Write < or > in each box.**

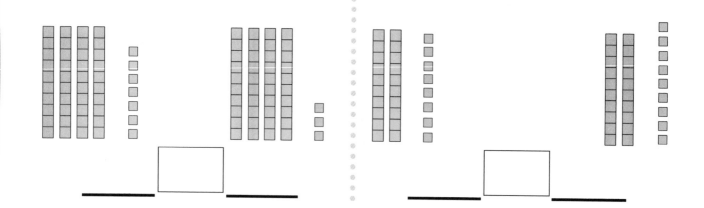

**Write the number that is just after or between.**

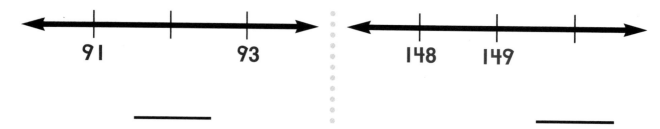

**Circle *even* or *odd* for each number.**

9          even          odd    16          even          odd

**Draw lines to match.**

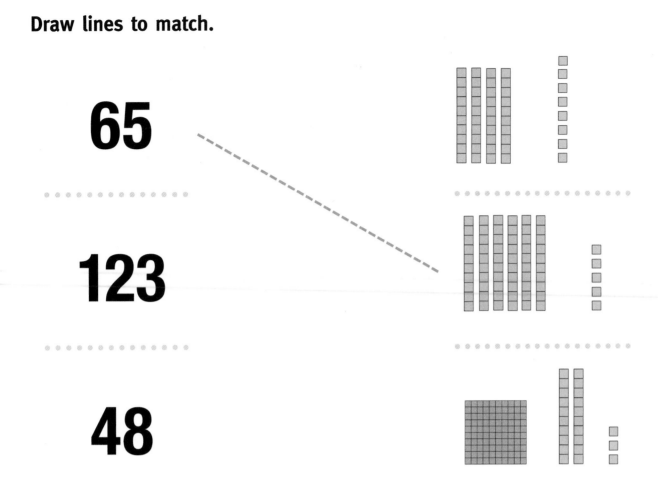

**65**

**123**

**48**

**Write the missing numbers in each row.**

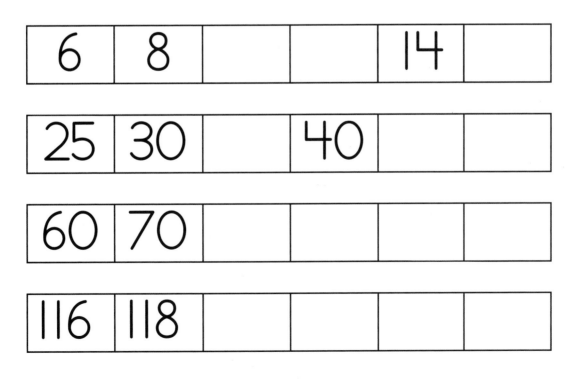

| 6 | 8 | | | 14 | |
|---|---|---|---|---|---|

| 25 | 30 | | 40 | | |
|----|----|---|----|---|---|

| 60 | 70 | | | | |
|----|----|---|---|---|---|

| 116 | 118 | | | | |
|-----|-----|---|---|---|---|

# unit 2
## Addition

## Sums to 10

Add.

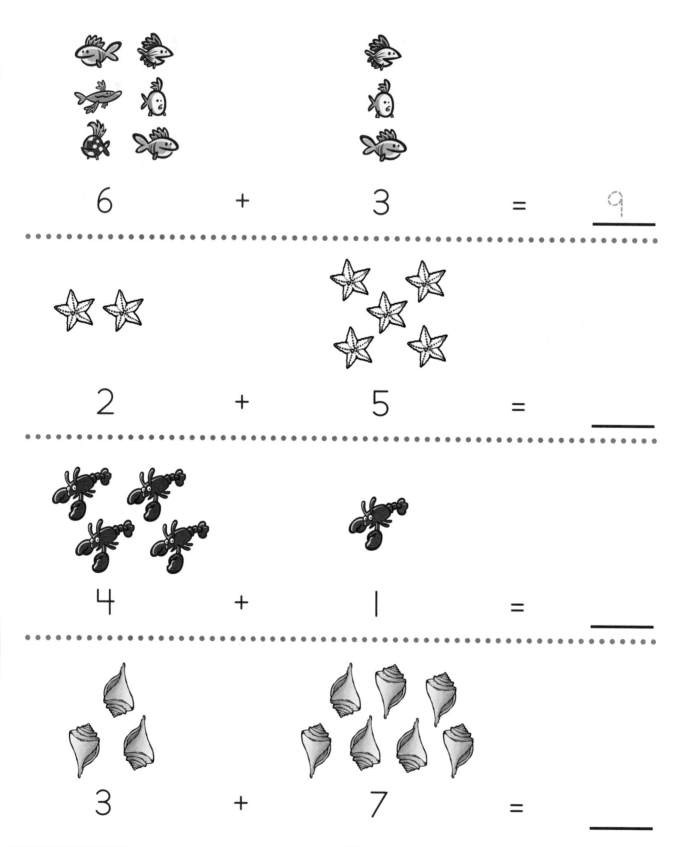

6     +     3     =     9

2     +     5     =     ___

4     +     1     =     ___

3     +     7     =     ___

# Sums to 10

Write the numbers that match the pictures. Then add.

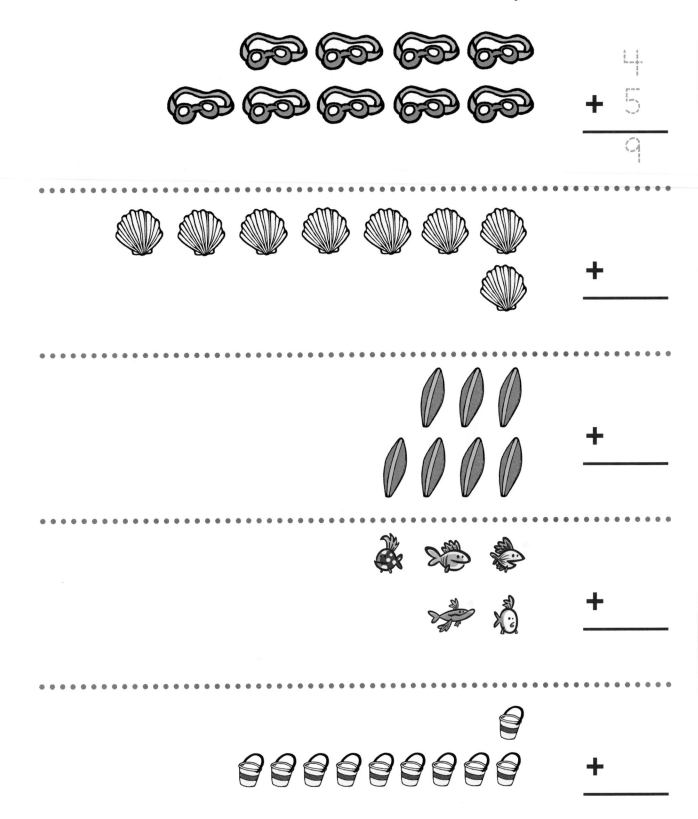

4
+ 5
___
9

+
___

+
___

+
___

+
___

# Sums to 18

**Add.**

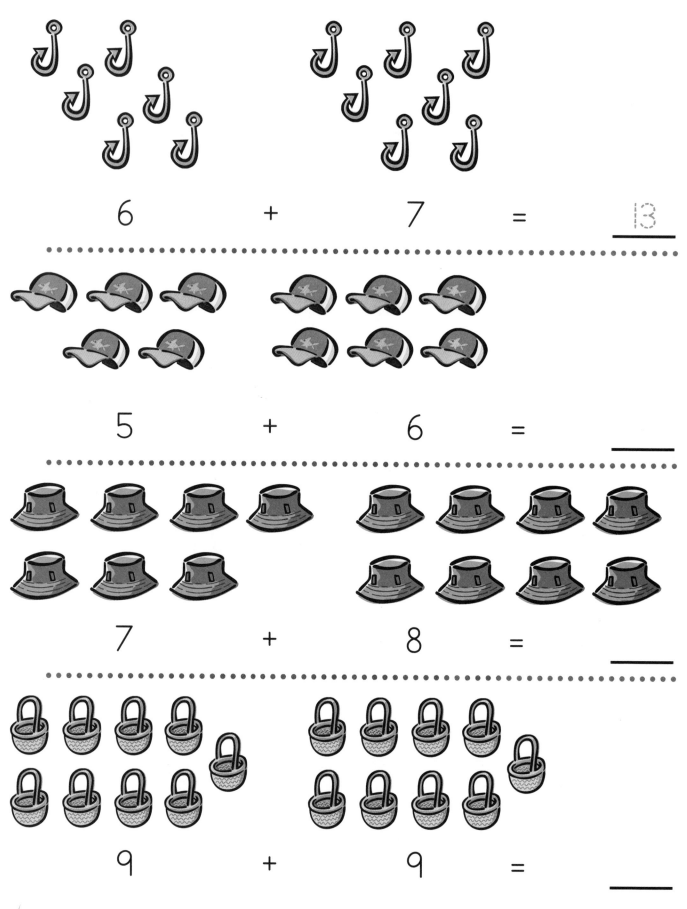

6 + 7 = 13

5 + 6 = _____

7 + 8 = _____

9 + 9 = _____

Write the numbers that match the pictures. Then add.

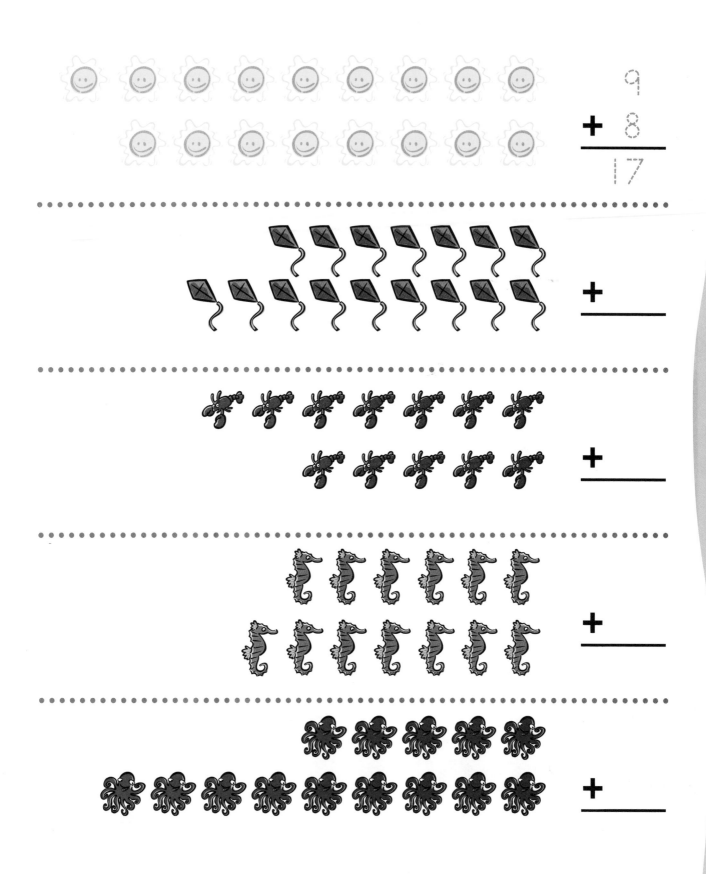

$$
\begin{array}{r}
9 \\
+\ 8 \\
\hline
17
\end{array}
$$

$+$ ____

$+$ ____

$+$ ____

$+$ ____

# Adding Zero

Write the numbers that match the pictures. Then add.

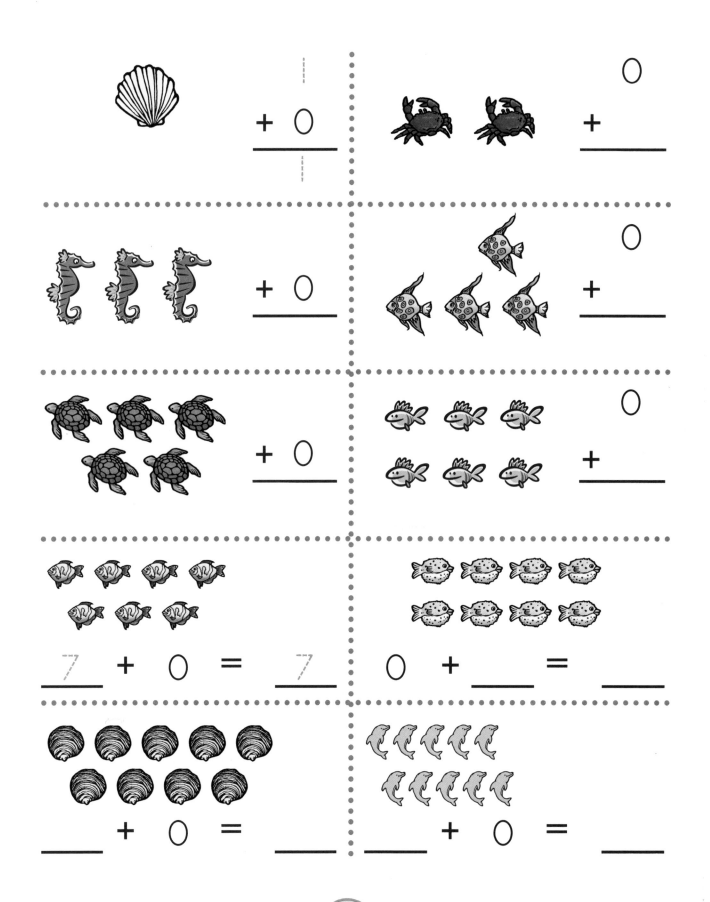

1

+ 0
___

0

+
___

+ 0
___

0

+
___

+ 0
___

0

+
___

7 + 0 = 7

0 + ___ = ___

___ + 0 = ___

___ + 0 = ___

# Doubles

Write the numbers that match the fish. Then add.

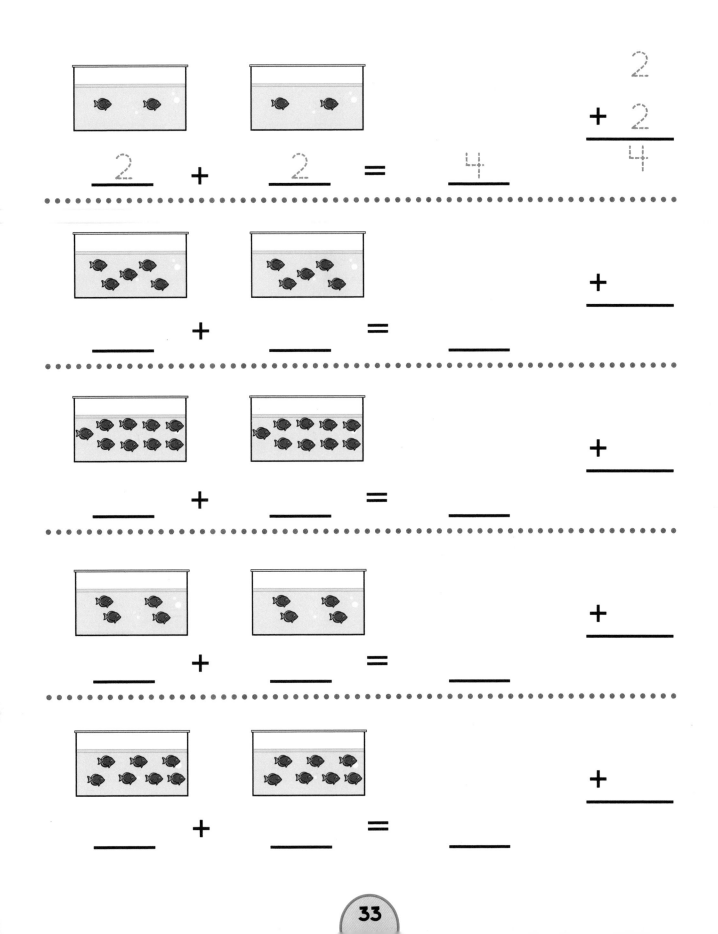

2 + 2 = 4

$$\begin{array}{r} 2 \\ +\ 2 \\ \hline 4 \end{array}$$

___ + ___ = ___

___ + ___ = ___

___ + ___ = ___

___ + ___ = ___

# Order Property

**Write the sums that match the cubes.**

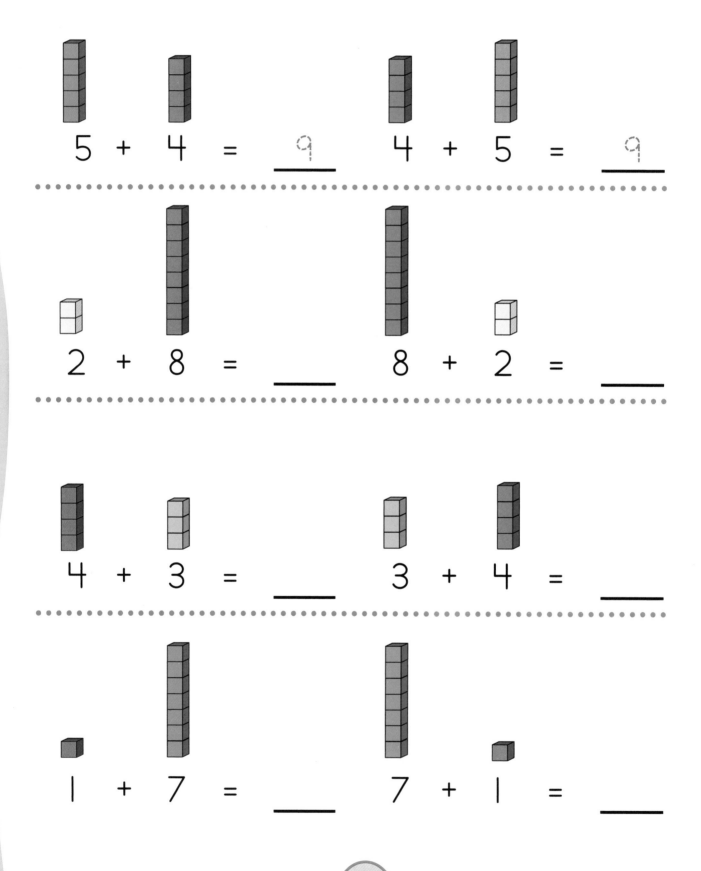

5 + 4 = 9

4 + 5 = 9

2 + 8 = ___

8 + 2 = ___

4 + 3 = ___

3 + 4 = ___

1 + 7 = ___

7 + 1 = ___

**Find the number of each object on the graph. Then write the sums.**

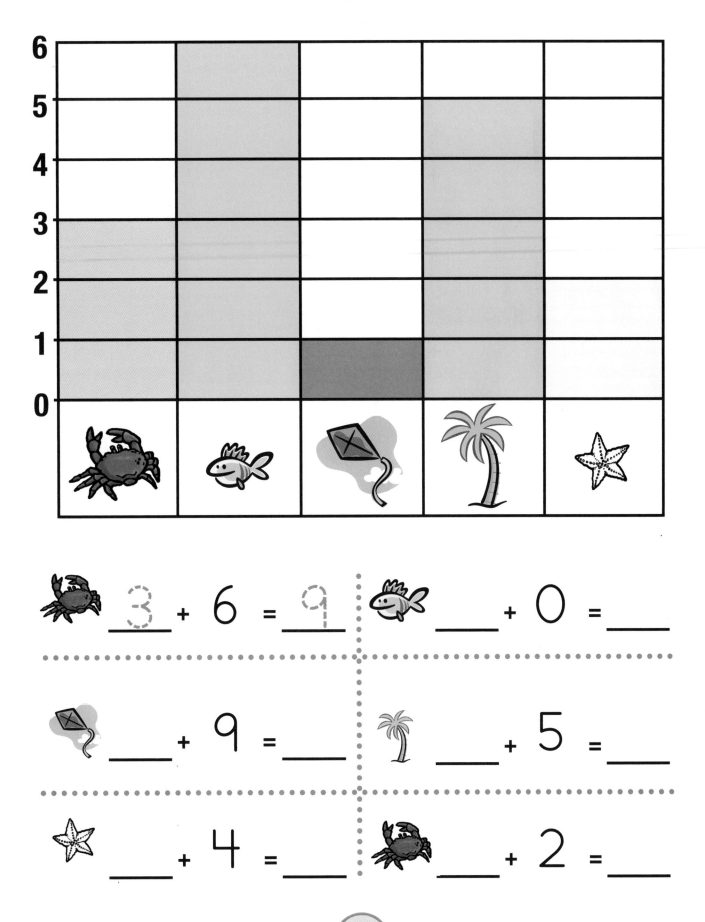

3 + 6 = 9

___ + 0 = ___

___ + 9 = ___

___ + 5 = ___

___ + 4 = ___

___ + 2 = ___

# Two-digit Addition

Combine the blocks. Then write the sums.

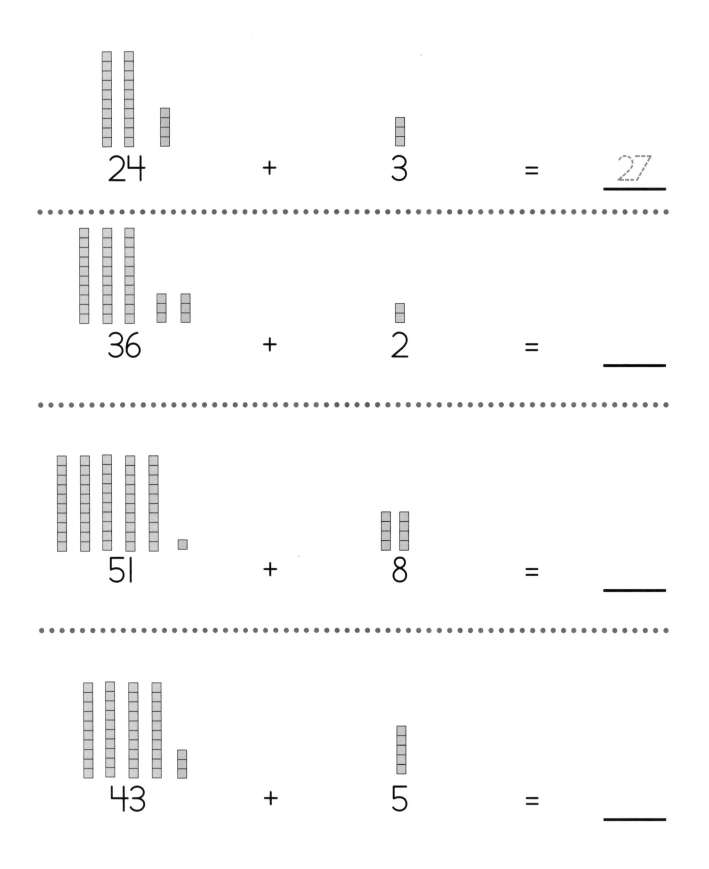

24    +    3    =    27

36    +    2    =    ____

51    +    8    =    ____

43    +    5    =    ____

# Two-digit Addition

**Combine the blocks. Then write the sums.**

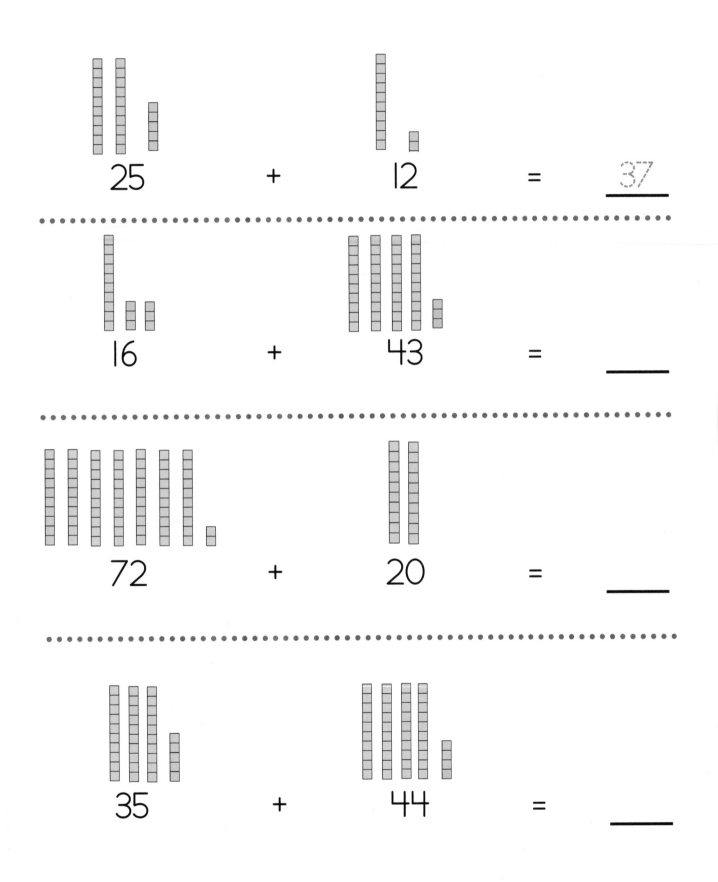

25    +    12    =    37

16    +    43    = _____

72    +    20    = _____

35    +    44    = _____

# Two-digit Addition

Use these steps to add two-digit numbers.

**Find: 86 + 1**

| Step 1 | Step 2 |
|---|---|
| Add the ones. | Add the tens. |
| (6 + 1 = 7) | (8 + 0 = 8) |

Step 1:
```
  T | O
  8 | 6
+   | 1
----+----
    | 7
```

Step 2:
```
  T | O
  8 | 6
+   | 1
----+----
  8 | 7
```

**Find: 26 + 53**

| Step 1 | Step 2 |
|---|---|
| Add the ones. | Add the tens. |
| (6 + 3 = 9) | (2 + 5 = 7) |

Step 1:
```
  T | O
  2 | 6
+ 5 | 3
----+----
    | 9
```

Step 2:
```
  T | O
  2 | 6
+ 5 | 3
----+----
  7 | 9
```

**Add.**

```
  T | O        T | O        T | O        T | O
  8 | 6        2 | 6        1 | 0        5 | 2
+   | 1      + 5 | 3      + 1 | 3      +   | 5
----+----    ----+----    ----+----    ----+----
  8 | 7        7 | 9        |            |
```

```
  T | O        T | O        T | O        T | O
  4 | 3        7 | 5        9 | 7        1 | 2
+ 1 | 3      + 1 | 0      +   | 2      + 4 | 2
----+----    ----+----    ----+----    ----+----
  |            |            |            |
```

```
  T | O        T | O        T | O        T | O
  8 | 0        2 | 3        3 | 2        6 | 3
+ 1 | 2      + 7 | 0      +   | 6      + 3 | 1
----+----    ----+----    ----+----    ----+----
  |            |            |            |
```

```
  T | O        T | O        T | O        T | O
  6 | 8        7 | 3        3 | 6        4 | 5
+ 2 | 1      +   | 6      + 1 | 2      + 4 | 4
----+----    ----+----    ----+----    ----+----
  |            |            |            |
```

### Add.

| | | | |
|---|---|---|---|
| 32<br>+  7<br>**39** | 46<br>+ 21 | 12<br>+ 42 | 13<br>+ 54 |
| 59<br>+ 10 | 75<br>+  3 | 63<br>+ 31 | 14<br>+ 82 |
| 40<br>+ 17 | 21<br>+  7 | 35<br>+ 31 | 50<br>+ 28 |
| 64<br>+  5 | 38<br>+ 20 | 14<br>+ 14 | 80<br>+  9 |
| 75<br>+ 23 | 19<br>+ 40 | 82<br>+  7 | 54<br>+ 22 |
| 16<br>+  3 | 48<br>+ 30 | 74<br>+ 11 | 50<br>+ 29 |

# Two-digit Addition

Shade each area with a sum of 89.

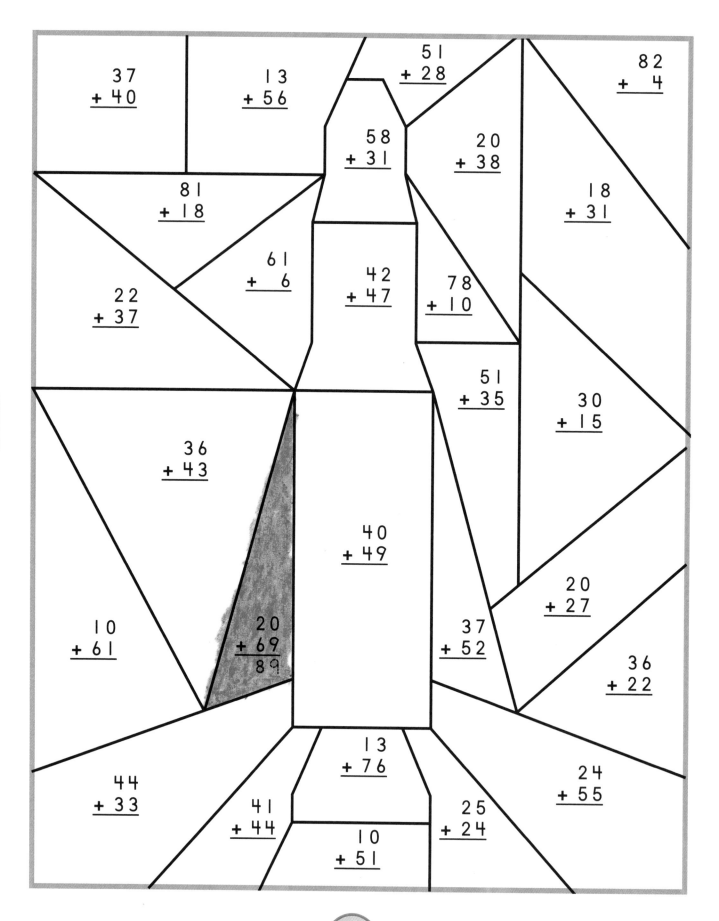

$$\begin{array}{r}37\\+40\\\hline\end{array}$$

$$\begin{array}{r}13\\+56\\\hline\end{array}$$

$$\begin{array}{r}51\\+28\\\hline\end{array}$$

$$\begin{array}{r}82\\+\ 4\\\hline\end{array}$$

$$\begin{array}{r}58\\+31\\\hline\end{array}$$

$$\begin{array}{r}20\\+38\\\hline\end{array}$$

$$\begin{array}{r}81\\+18\\\hline\end{array}$$

$$\begin{array}{r}18\\+31\\\hline\end{array}$$

$$\begin{array}{r}61\\+\ 6\\\hline\end{array}$$

$$\begin{array}{r}42\\+47\\\hline\end{array}$$

$$\begin{array}{r}78\\+10\\\hline\end{array}$$

$$\begin{array}{r}22\\+37\\\hline\end{array}$$

$$\begin{array}{r}51\\+35\\\hline\end{array}$$

$$\begin{array}{r}30\\+15\\\hline\end{array}$$

$$\begin{array}{r}36\\+43\\\hline\end{array}$$

$$\begin{array}{r}40\\+49\\\hline\end{array}$$

$$\begin{array}{r}20\\+27\\\hline\end{array}$$

$$\begin{array}{r}10\\+61\\\hline\end{array}$$

$$\begin{array}{r}20\\+69\\\hline 89\end{array}$$

$$\begin{array}{r}37\\+52\\\hline\end{array}$$

$$\begin{array}{r}36\\+22\\\hline\end{array}$$

$$\begin{array}{r}13\\+76\\\hline\end{array}$$

$$\begin{array}{r}24\\+55\\\hline\end{array}$$

$$\begin{array}{r}44\\+33\\\hline\end{array}$$

$$\begin{array}{r}41\\+44\\\hline\end{array}$$

$$\begin{array}{r}25\\+24\\\hline\end{array}$$

$$\begin{array}{r}10\\+51\\\hline\end{array}$$

# Three-digit Addition

Combine the blocks. Then write the sums.

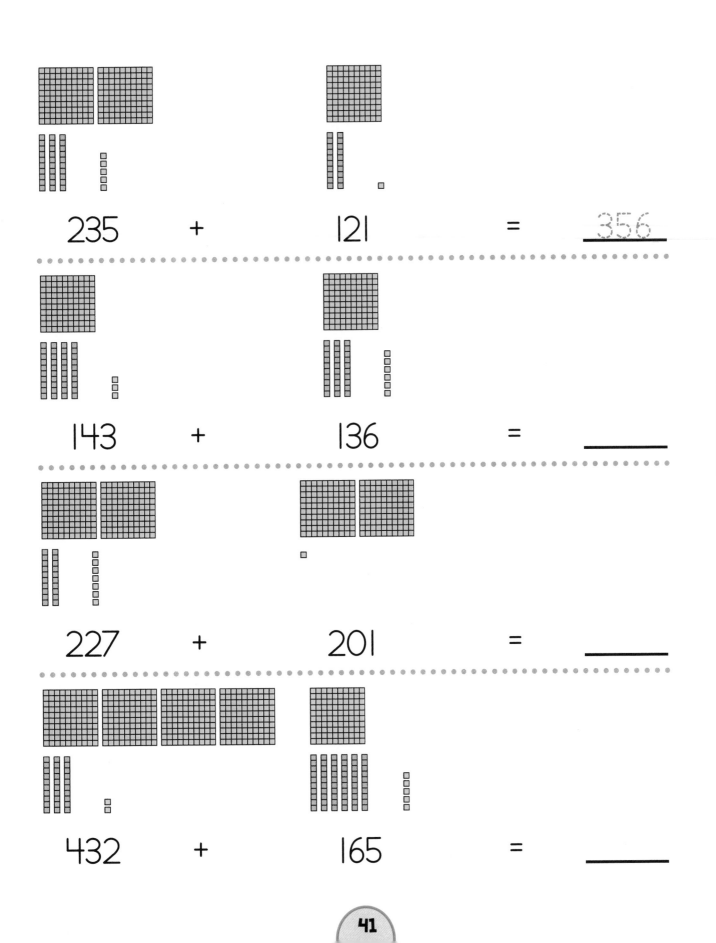

235    +    121    =    356

143    +    136    =    _____

227    +    201    =    _____

432    +    165    =    _____

# Three-digit Addition

Use these steps to add three-digit numbers.

Find: 301 + 375

| **Step 1** | **Step 2** | **Step 3** |
|---|---|---|
| Add the ones. | Add the tens. | Add the hundreds. |
| (1 + 5 = 6) | (0 + 7 = 7) | (3 + 3 = 6) |

| H | T | O |
|---|---|---|
| 3 | 0 | 1 |
| + 3 | 7 | 5 |
| | | 6 |

| H | T | O |
|---|---|---|
| 3 | 0 | 1 |
| + 3 | 7 | 5 |
| | 7 | 6 |

| H | T | O |
|---|---|---|
| 3 | 0 | 1 |
| + 3 | 7 | 5 |
| 6 | 7 | 6 |

**Add.**

| H | T | O |
|---|---|---|
| 2 | 4 | 3 |
| + 3 | 2 | 5 |
| 5 | 6 | 8 |

| H | T | O |
|---|---|---|
| 4 | 1 | 0 |
| + 4 | 4 | 6 |
| | | |

| H | T | O |
|---|---|---|
| 3 | 3 | 2 |
| + 4 | 2 | 7 |
| | | |

| H | T | O |
|---|---|---|
| 2 | 0 | 6 |
| + 7 | 5 | 1 |
| | | |

| H | T | O |
|---|---|---|
| 6 | 2 | 1 |
| + 3 | 5 | 0 |
| | | |

| H | T | O |
|---|---|---|
| 1 | 7 | 6 |
| + 3 | 0 | 2 |
| | | |

| H | T | O |
|---|---|---|
| 2 | 4 | 0 |
| + 1 | 2 | 3 |
| | | |

| H | T | O |
|---|---|---|
| 1 | 5 | 2 |
| + 8 | 4 | 7 |
| | | |

| H | T | O |
|---|---|---|
| 7 | 0 | 1 |
| + 1 | 1 | 1 |
| | | |

| H | T | O |
|---|---|---|
| 5 | 4 | 2 |
| + 3 | 1 | 0 |
| | | |

| H | T | O |
|---|---|---|
| 7 | 1 | 2 |
| + 2 | 0 | 3 |
| | | |

| H | T | O |
|---|---|---|
| 2 | 0 | 2 |
| + 4 | 1 | 4 |
| | | |

**Regroup 10 ones as 1 ten. Then write the regrouped numbers.**

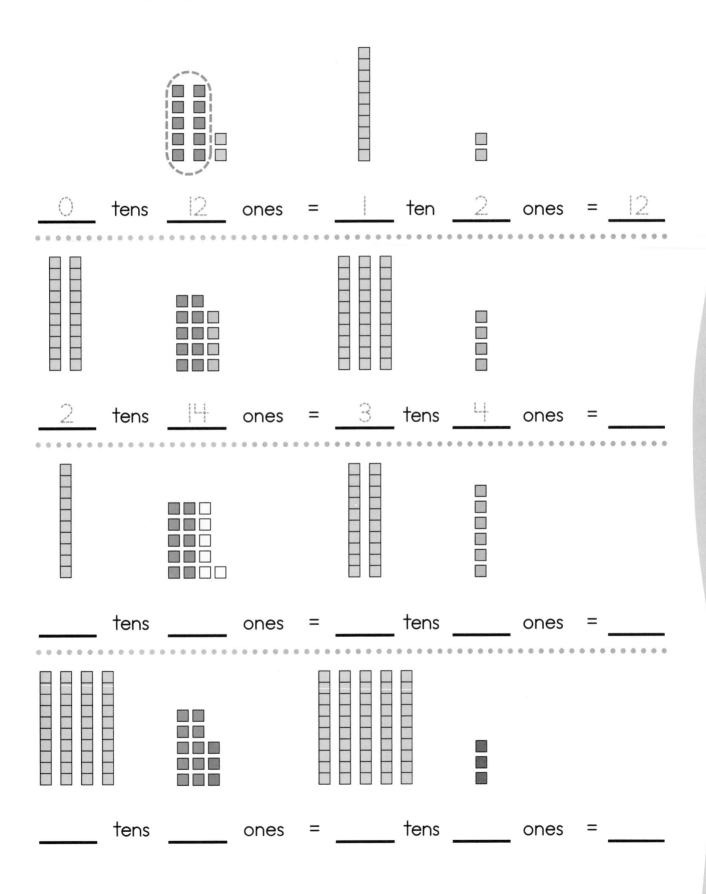

__0__ tens __12__ ones = __1__ ten __2__ ones = __12__

__2__ tens __14__ ones = __3__ tens __4__ ones = _____

_____ tens _____ ones = _____ tens _____ ones = _____

_____ tens _____ ones = _____ tens _____ ones = _____

43

# Two-digit Addition, Regrouping Ones

**Regroup the ones. Write the sums.**

## 15 + 8

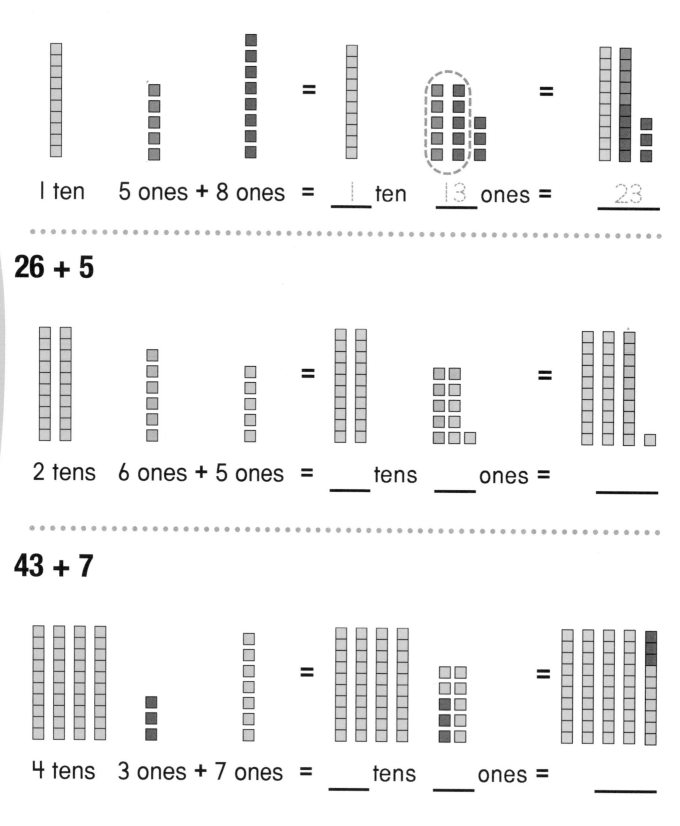

1 ten    5 ones + 8 ones = __1__ ten    _13_ ones = _23_

## 26 + 5

2 tens    6 ones + 5 ones = ___ tens ___ ones = ___

## 43 + 7

4 tens    3 ones + 7 ones = ___ tens ___ ones = ___

# Two-digit Addition, Regrouping Ones

Use these steps to add two digits, regrouping ones.

**Find: 34 + 38**

| Step 1 | Step 2 |
|---|---|
| Add the ones. | Add the tens. |
| (4 + 8 = 12) | (1 + 3 + 3 = 7) |
| Regroup as 1 ten and 2 ones. | |

Step 1:
```
  [1]
  T | O
  3 | 4
+ 3 | 8
    | 2
```

Step 2:
```
  [1]
  T | O
  3 | 4
+ 3 | 8
  7 | 2
```

**Add.**

```
  [1]              [ ]              [ ]              [ ]
  T | O            T | O            T | O            T | O
  3 | 7            1 | 2            6 | 5            5 | 4
+ 2 | 8          + 3 | 8          + 1 | 7          + 2 | 6
  6   5
```

```
  [ ]              [ ]              [ ]              [ ]
  T | O            T | O            T | O            T | O
  1 | 2            4 | 6            3 | 3            1 | 5
+ 2 | 9          + 4 | 5          + 1 | 7          + 1 | 8
```

```
  [ ]              [ ]              [ ]              [ ]
  T | O            T | O            T | O            T | O
  5 | 7            4 | 3            1 | 7            6 | 9
+ 2 | 3          + 2 | 9          + 7 | 4          + 2 | 9
```

# Two-digit Addition, Regrouping Ones

Add.

| | | T | O |
|---|---|---|---|
| | | 5 | 7 |
| + | | | 6 |
| | | 6 | 3 |

[box: 1]

| | | T | O |
|---|---|---|---|
| | | 2 | 9 |
| + | | 3 | 7 |

[box: blank]

| | | T | O |
|---|---|---|---|
| | | 3 | 6 |
| + | | 4 | 4 |

| | | T | O |
|---|---|---|---|
| | | 2 | 4 |
| + | | 1 | 8 |

| | | T | O |
|---|---|---|---|
| | | 5 | 9 |
| + | | 1 | 2 |

| | | T | O |
|---|---|---|---|
| | | 5 | 7 |
| + | | | 8 |

| | | T | O |
|---|---|---|---|
| | | 1 | 9 |
| + | | 3 | 1 |

| | | T | O |
|---|---|---|---|
| | | 2 | 9 |
| + | | 4 | 6 |

| | | T | O |
|---|---|---|---|
| | | 2 | 9 |
| + | | 5 | 5 |

| | | T | O |
|---|---|---|---|
| | | 1 | 8 |
| + | | 5 | 2 |

| | | T | O |
|---|---|---|---|
| | | 4 | 6 |
| + | | 4 | 4 |

| | | T | O |
|---|---|---|---|
| | | 1 | 9 |
| + | | | 6 |

| | | T | O |
|---|---|---|---|
| | | 1 | 8 |
| + | | 6 | 3 |

| | | T | O |
|---|---|---|---|
| | | 2 | 9 |
| + | | | 2 |

| | | T | O |
|---|---|---|---|
| | | 4 | 8 |
| + | | 1 | 4 |

| | | T | O |
|---|---|---|---|
| | | 1 | 9 |
| + | | 1 | 1 |

# Two-digit Addition, Regrouping Ones

**Match the problems to their sums.**

| ☐ | ☐ | ☐ | ☐ | ☐ |
|---|---|---|---|---|
| 16 | 36 | 14 | 27 | 17 |
| + 67 | + 36 | + 6 | + 46 | + 47 |

83

| 72 | 83 | 73 | 20 | 64 |
|---|---|---|---|---|

| ☐ | ☐ | ☐ | ☐ | ☐ |
|---|---|---|---|---|
| 37 | 14 | 16 | 55 | 27 |
| + 29 | + 77 | + 38 | + 5 | + 38 |

| 66 | 54 | 91 | 65 | 60 |
|---|---|---|---|---|

| ☐ | ☐ | ☐ | ☐ | ☐ |
|---|---|---|---|---|
| 35 | 27 | 75 | 22 | 66 |
| + 17 | + 3 | + 19 | + 68 | + 9 |

| 30 | 52 | 94 | 75 | 90 |
|---|---|---|---|---|

| ☐ | ☐ | ☐ | ☐ | ☐ |
|---|---|---|---|---|
| 12 | 64 | 77 | 27 | 61 |
| + 59 | + 18 | + 6 | + 14 | + 29 |

| 82 | 71 | 41 | 83 | 90 |
|---|---|---|---|---|

# Two-digit Addition, Regrouping Ones

Shade each box that has a sum of 72.

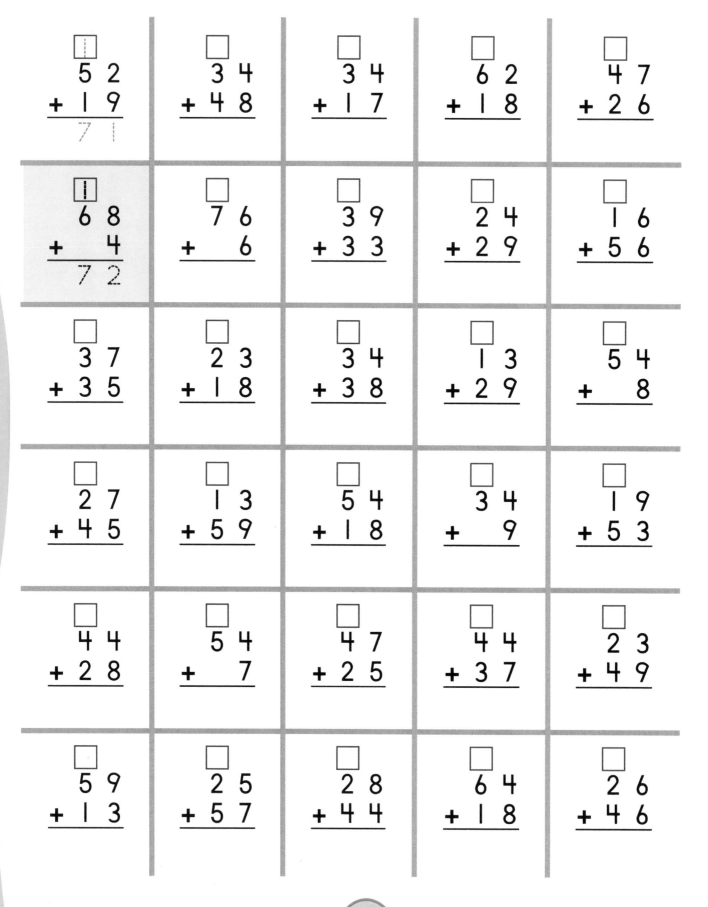

| □ | □ | □ | □ | □ |
|---|---|---|---|---|
| 5 2 | 3 4 | 3 4 | 6 2 | 4 7 |
| + 1 9 | + 4 8 | + 1 7 | + 1 8 | + 2 6 |
| 7 1 | | | | |

| 1 | □ | □ | □ | □ |
|---|---|---|---|---|
| 6 8 | 7 6 | 3 9 | 2 4 | 1 6 |
| + 4 | + 6 | + 3 3 | + 2 9 | + 5 6 |
| 7 2 | | | | |

| □ | □ | □ | □ | □ |
|---|---|---|---|---|
| 3 7 | 2 3 | 3 4 | 1 3 | 5 4 |
| + 3 5 | + 1 8 | + 3 8 | + 2 9 | + 8 |

| □ | □ | □ | □ | □ |
|---|---|---|---|---|
| 2 7 | 1 3 | 5 4 | 3 4 | 1 9 |
| + 4 5 | + 5 9 | + 1 8 | + 9 | + 5 3 |

| □ | □ | □ | □ | □ |
|---|---|---|---|---|
| 4 4 | 5 4 | 4 7 | 4 4 | 2 3 |
| + 2 8 | + 7 | + 2 5 | + 3 7 | + 4 9 |

| □ | □ | □ | □ | □ |
|---|---|---|---|---|
| 5 9 | 2 5 | 2 8 | 6 4 | 2 6 |
| + 1 3 | + 5 7 | + 4 4 | + 1 8 | + 4 6 |

# Use Estimation

Change each number to the closest ten.
Then circle the best estimate for the sum.

13 + 29

_10_ + _30_

30    (40)    50

---

61 + 19

___ + ___

60    70    80

---

37 + 8

___ + ___

50    60    70

---

11 + 48

___ + ___

50    60    70

---

22 + 31

___ + ___

40    50    60

---

47 + 29

___ + ___

70    80    90

---

12 + 12

___ + ___

10    20    30

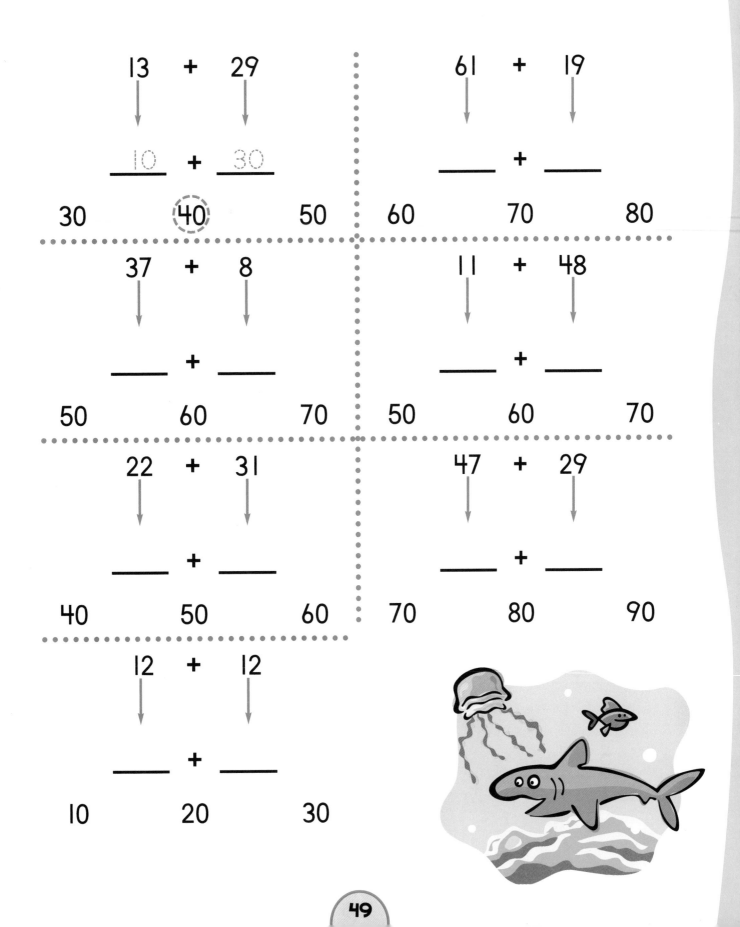

**Add.**

$$6 + 2 = \underline{\phantom{00}} \qquad 4 + 5 = \underline{\phantom{00}}$$

$$9 + 7 = \underline{\phantom{00}} \qquad 8 + 6 = \underline{\phantom{00}}$$

$$0 + 10 = \underline{\phantom{00}} \qquad 9 + 9 = \underline{\phantom{00}}$$

$$8 + 8 = \underline{\phantom{00}} \qquad 3 + 9 = \underline{\phantom{00}}$$

$$\begin{array}{r} 1\,6 \\ +\ \ 3 \\ \hline \end{array} \qquad \begin{array}{r} 2\,5 \\ +\,4\,1 \\ \hline \end{array} \qquad \begin{array}{r} 3\,2 \\ +\,6\,2 \\ \hline \end{array} \qquad \begin{array}{r} 1\,8 \\ +\,5\,1 \\ \hline \end{array}$$

$$\begin{array}{r} 3\,0 \\ +\ \ 9 \\ \hline \end{array} \qquad \begin{array}{r} 4\,7 \\ +\,1\,1 \\ \hline \end{array} \qquad \begin{array}{r} 3\,5 \\ +\,2\,3 \\ \hline \end{array} \qquad \begin{array}{r} 8\,3 \\ +\,1\,4 \\ \hline \end{array}$$

$$\begin{array}{r} 4\,0\,3 \\ +\,1\,6\,3 \\ \hline \end{array} \qquad \begin{array}{r} 5\,2\,1 \\ +\,1\,4\,0 \\ \hline \end{array} \qquad \begin{array}{r} 6\,3\,2 \\ +\,3\,0\,5 \\ \hline \end{array} \qquad \begin{array}{r} 2\,8\,5 \\ +\,2\,1\,4 \\ \hline \end{array}$$

$$\begin{array}{r} \Box \\ 1\,5 \\ +\ \ 6 \\ \hline \end{array} \qquad \begin{array}{r} \Box \\ 3\,8 \\ +\,3\,5 \\ \hline \end{array} \qquad \begin{array}{r} \Box \\ 2\,9 \\ +\,1\,8 \\ \hline \end{array} \qquad \begin{array}{r} \Box \\ 3\,7 \\ +\,2\,4 \\ \hline \end{array}$$

$$\begin{array}{r} \Box \\ 5\,8 \\ +\,1\,7 \\ \hline \end{array} \qquad \begin{array}{r} \Box \\ 2\,9 \\ +\,2\,9 \\ \hline \end{array} \qquad \begin{array}{r} \Box \\ 8\,8 \\ +\ \ 6 \\ \hline \end{array} \qquad \begin{array}{r} \Box \\ 4\,5 \\ +\,3\,8 \\ \hline \end{array}$$

# Unit 2 Review

**Find the number of each object on the graph.**
**Then write the sums.**

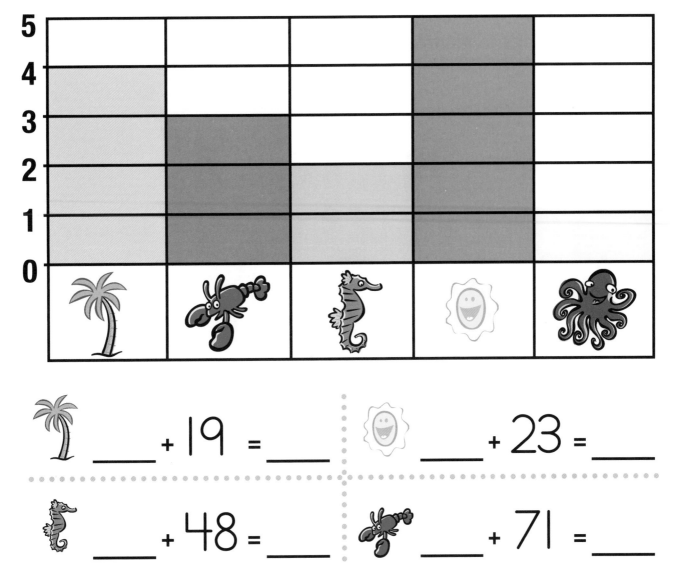

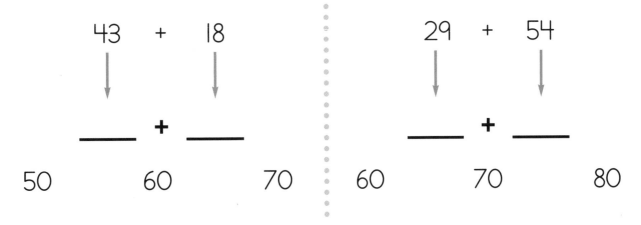

__ + 19 = __  __ + 23 = __

__ + 48 = __  __ + 71 = __

**Circle the best estimate for each sum.**

43 + 18  29 + 54

↓  ↓  ↓  ↓

__ + __  __ + __

50   60   70  60   70   80

# Differences from 10

**Cross out the dogs to subtract. Then write the differences.**

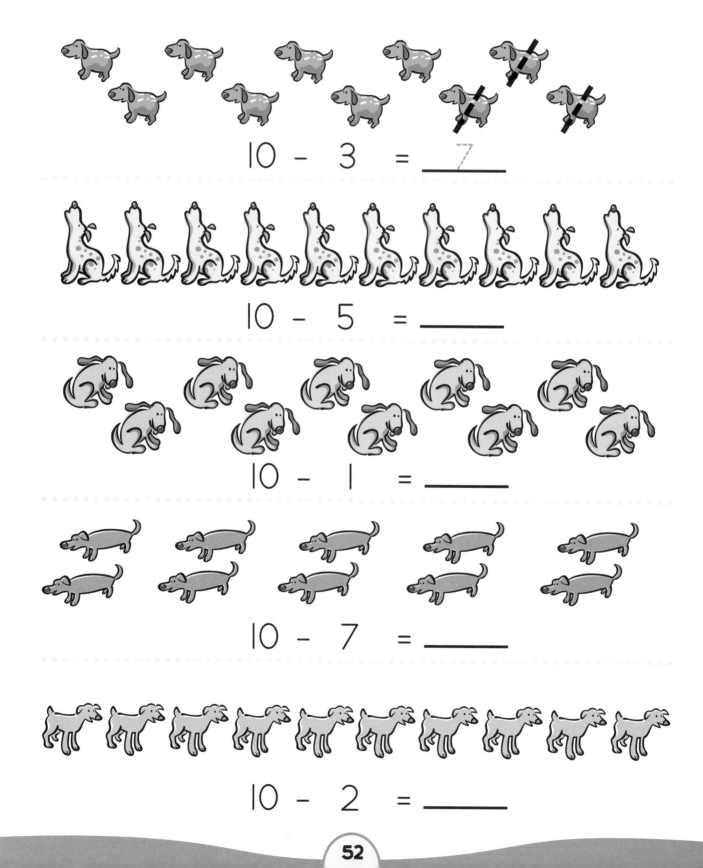

10 − 3 = __7__

10 − 5 = _____

10 − 1 = _____

10 − 7 = _____

10 − 2 = _____

Cross out the cats to subtract. Then write the differences.

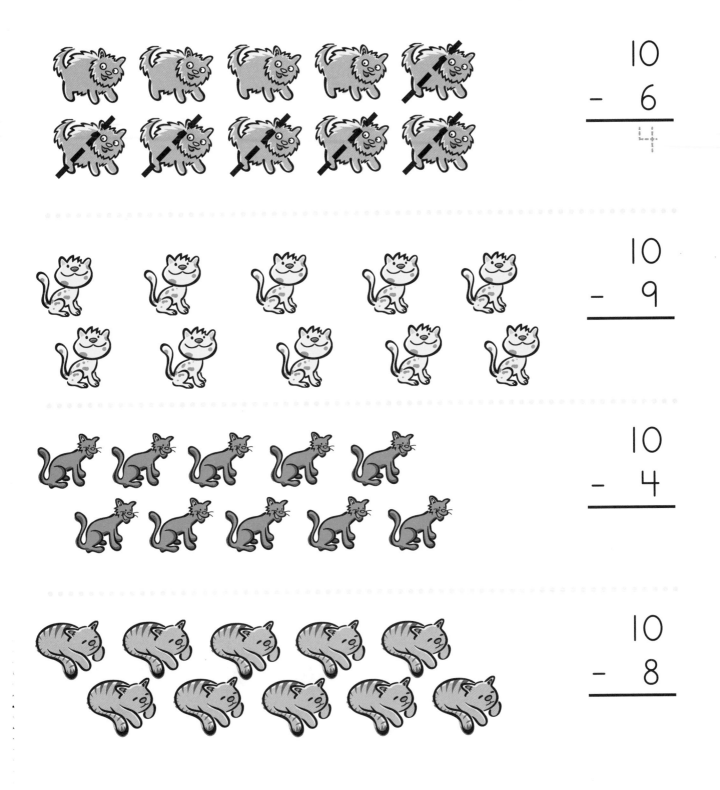

10
− 6
____
4

10
− 9
____

10
− 4
____

10
− 8
____

# Differences from 18

Cross out the rabbits to subtract. Then write the differences.

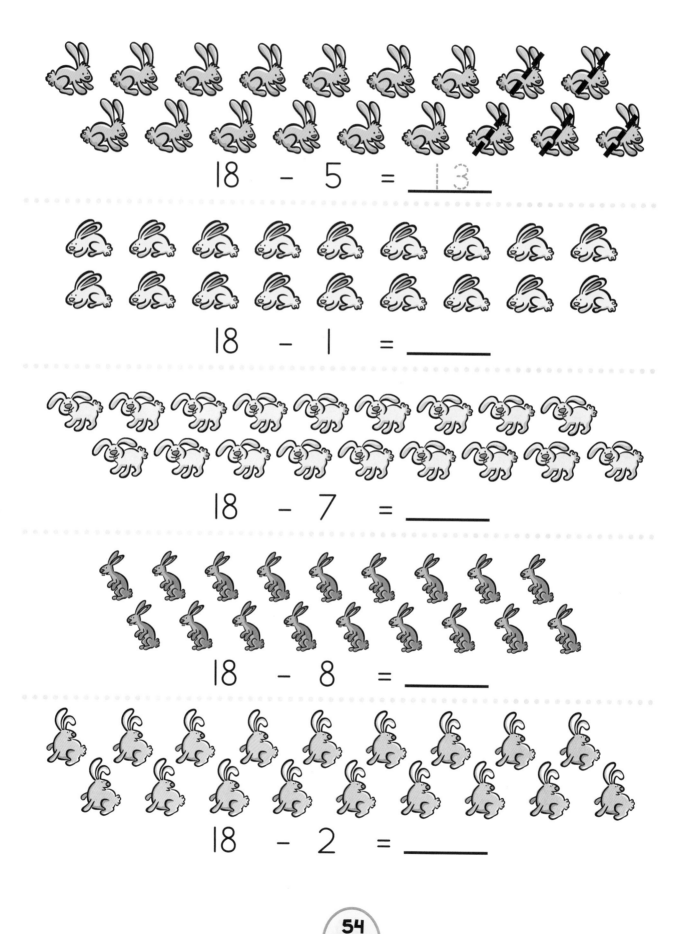

$$18 - 5 = \underline{13}$$

$$18 - 1 = \underline{\hphantom{00}}$$

$$18 - 7 = \underline{\hphantom{00}}$$

$$18 - 8 = \underline{\hphantom{00}}$$

$$18 - 2 = \underline{\hphantom{00}}$$

Cross out the animals to subtract. Then write the differences.

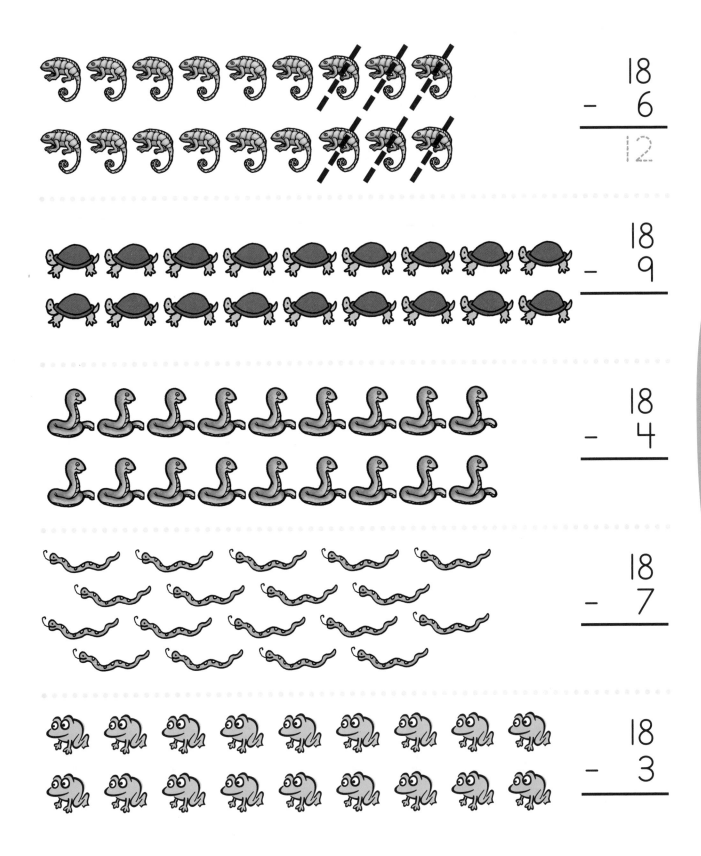

$$18 - 6 = 12$$

$$18 - 9$$

$$18 - 4$$

$$18 - 7$$

$$18 - 3$$

# Subtracting All

Write how many animals. Then subtract.

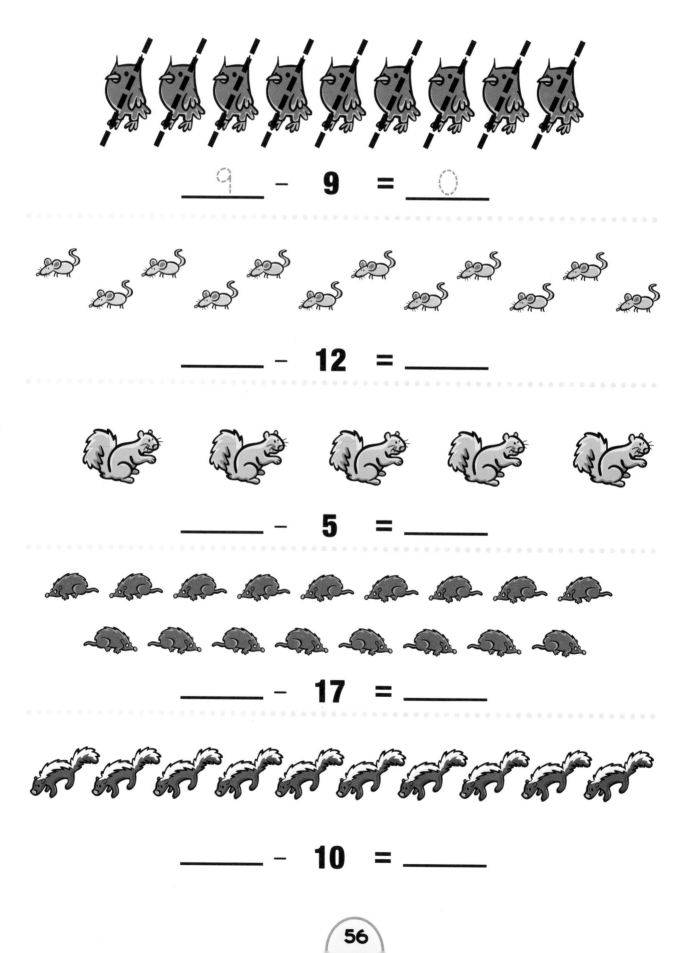

_9_ – **9** = _0_

_____ – **12** = _____

_____ – **5** = _____

_____ – **17** = _____

_____ – **10** = _____

# Subtracting Zero

**Write how many animals. Then subtract.**

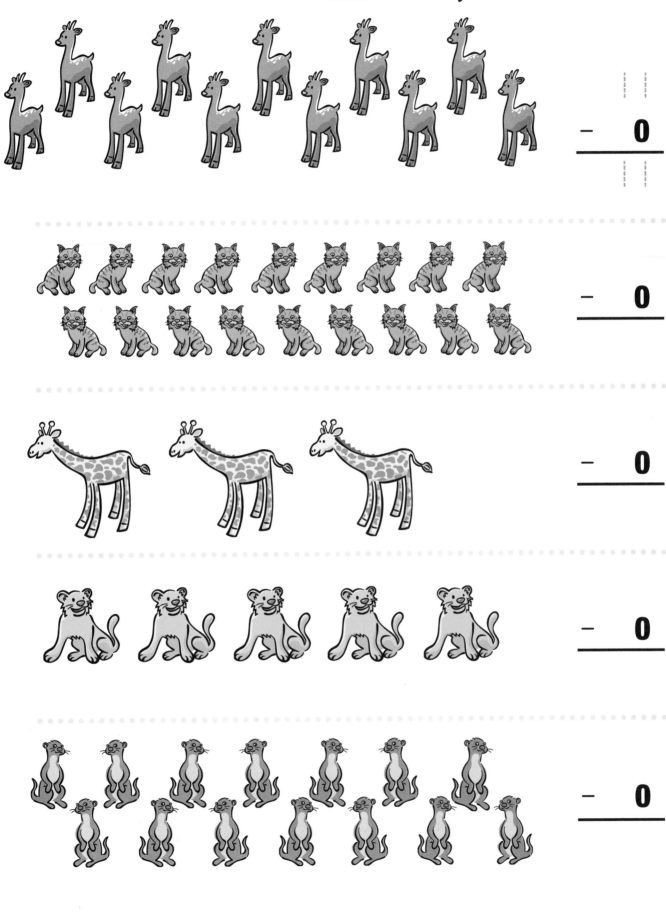

$$- \quad 0$$

$$- \quad 0$$

$$- \quad 0$$

$$- \quad 0$$

$$- \quad 0$$

57

# Order Property

Write the numbers to match the cubes.

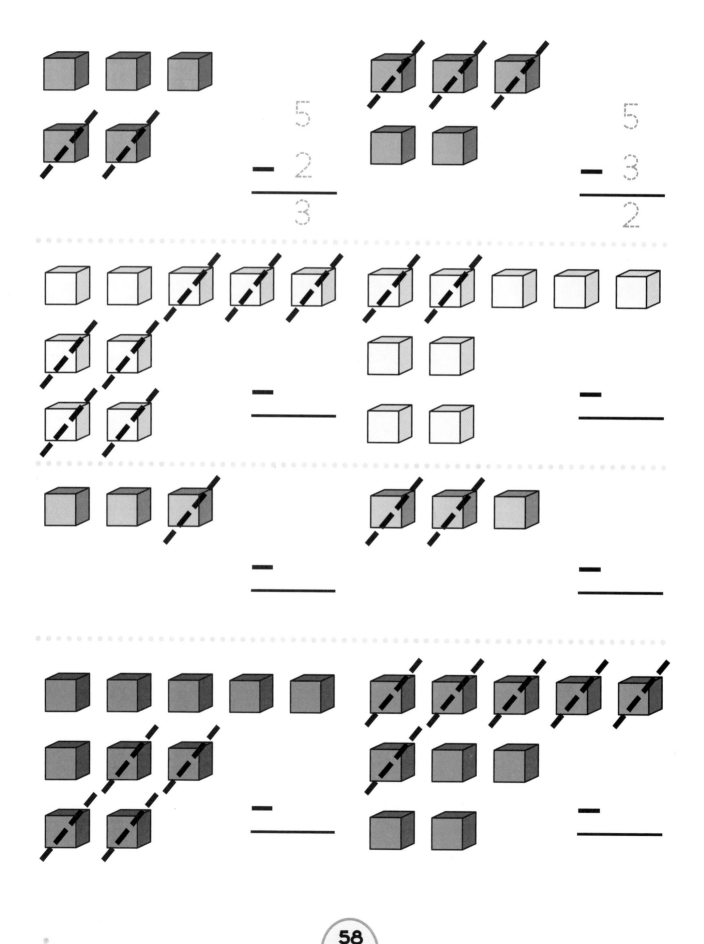

# Fact Families

Write the fact family for each set of numbers.

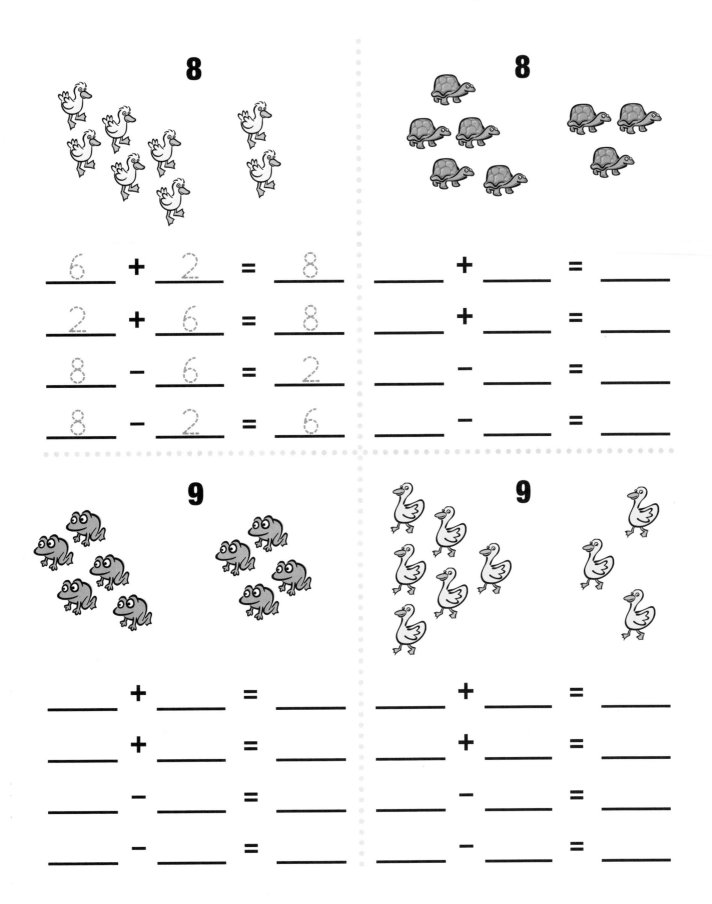

**8**

6 + 2 = 8

2 + 6 = 8

8 - 6 = 2

8 - 2 = 6

**8**

___ + ___ = ___

___ + ___ = ___

___ - ___ = ___

___ - ___ = ___

**9**

___ + ___ = ___

___ + ___ = ___

___ - ___ = ___

___ - ___ = ___

**9**

___ + ___ = ___

___ + ___ = ___

___ - ___ = ___

___ - ___ = ___

# Write a Number Sentence

Write the number sentences to match the pictures.

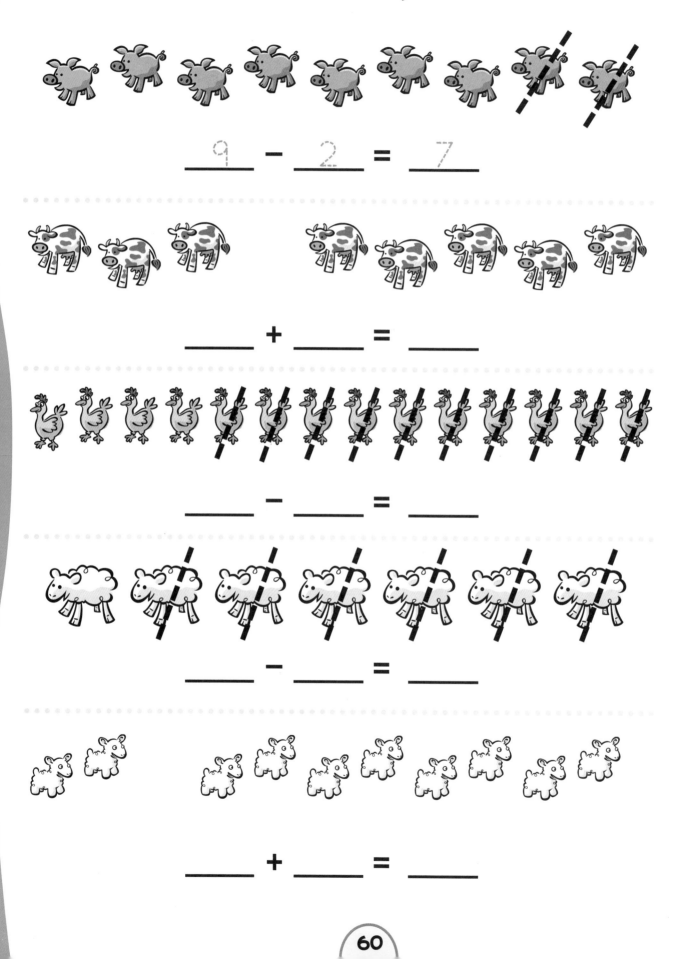

_____9_____ − _____2_____ = _____7_____

_____ + _____ = _____

_____ − _____ = _____

_____ − _____ = _____

_____ + _____ = _____

# Write a Number Sentence
### Write the number sentences to match the pictures.

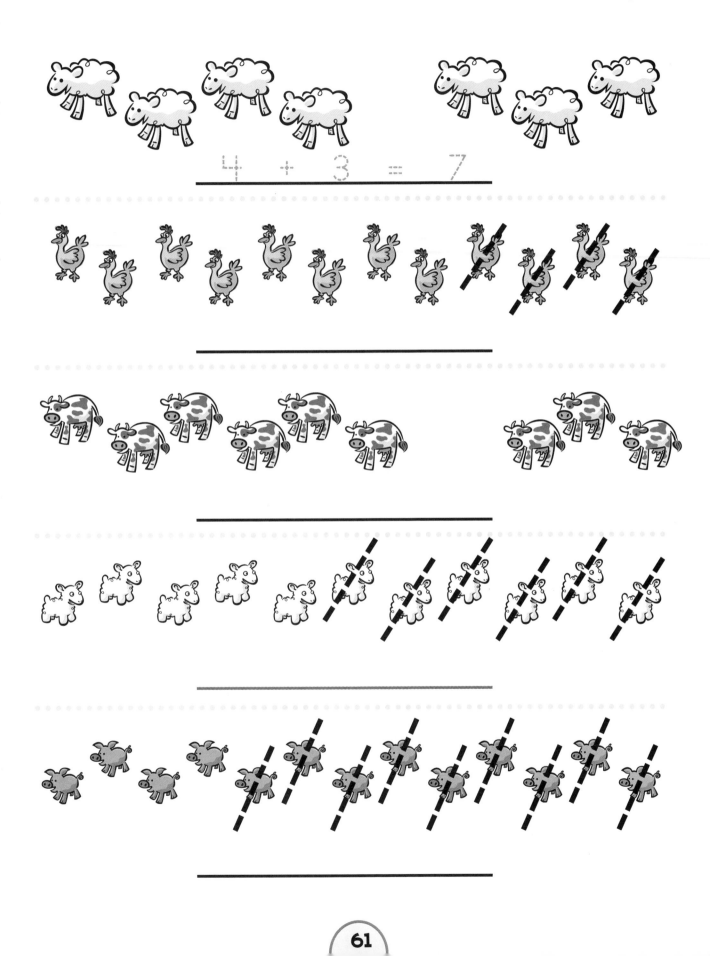

4 + 3 = 7

_____

_____

_____

_____

_____

# Two-digit Subtraction

Cross out ones to subtract.

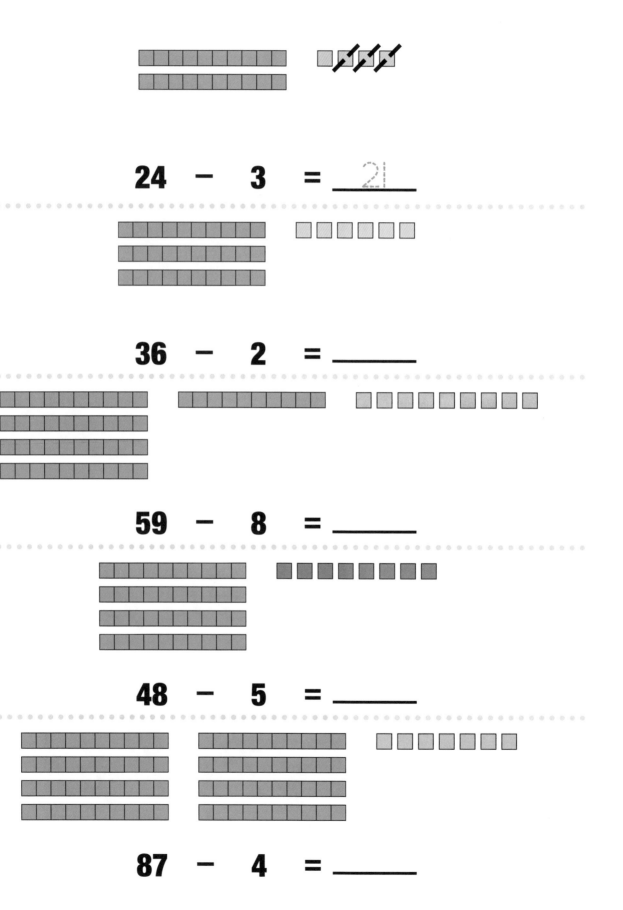

$24 - 3 = \underline{21}$

$36 - 2 = \underline{\phantom{00}}$

$59 - 8 = \underline{\phantom{00}}$

$48 - 5 = \underline{\phantom{00}}$

$87 - 4 = \underline{\phantom{00}}$

$$25 - 10 = \underline{15}$$

$$42 - 20 = \underline{\hspace{2cm}}$$

$$63 - 40 = \underline{\hspace{2cm}}$$

$$47 - 30 = \underline{\hspace{2cm}}$$

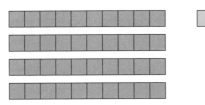

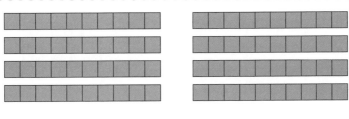

$$81 - 60 = \underline{\hspace{2cm}}$$

# Two-digit Subtraction

Cross out tens and ones to subtract.

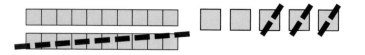

$$25 - 13 = \underline{12}$$

$$46 - 24 = \underline{\qquad}$$

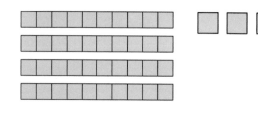

$$72 - 31 = \underline{\qquad}$$

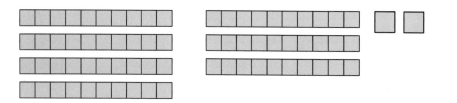

$$46 - 15 = \underline{\qquad}$$

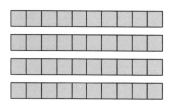

$$78 - 56 = \underline{\qquad}$$

# Two-digit Subtraction

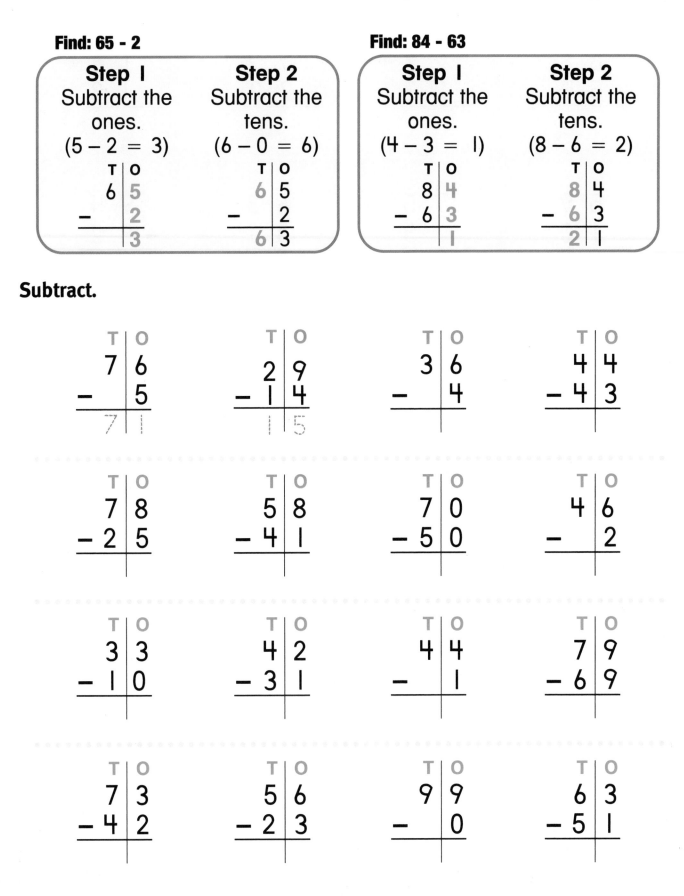

**Find: 65 - 2**

| Step 1 | Step 2 |
|---|---|
| Subtract the ones. (5 – 2 = 3) | Subtract the tens. (6 – 0 = 6) |

| T | O |
|---|---|
| 6 | 5 |
| – | 2 |
|   | 3 |

| T | O |
|---|---|
| 6 | 5 |
| – | 2 |
| 6 | 3 |

**Find: 84 - 63**

| Step 1 | Step 2 |
|---|---|
| Subtract the ones. (4 – 3 = 1) | Subtract the tens. (8 – 6 = 2) |

| T | O |
|---|---|
| 8 | 4 |
| – 6 | 3 |
|   | 1 |

| T | O |
|---|---|
| 8 | 4 |
| – 6 | 3 |
| 2 | 1 |

**Subtract.**

| T | O |
|---|---|
| 7 | 6 |
| – | 5 |
| 7 | 1 |

| T | O |
|---|---|
| 2 | 9 |
| – 1 | 4 |
| 1 | 5 |

| T | O |
|---|---|
| 3 | 6 |
| – | 4 |
|   |   |

| T | O |
|---|---|
| 4 | 4 |
| – 4 | 3 |
|   |   |

| T | O |
|---|---|
| 7 | 8 |
| – 2 | 5 |
|   |   |

| T | O |
|---|---|
| 5 | 8 |
| – 4 | 1 |
|   |   |

| T | O |
|---|---|
| 7 | 0 |
| – 5 | 0 |
|   |   |

| T | O |
|---|---|
| 4 | 6 |
| – | 2 |
|   |   |

| T | O |
|---|---|
| 3 | 3 |
| – 1 | 0 |
|   |   |

| T | O |
|---|---|
| 4 | 2 |
| – 3 | 1 |
|   |   |

| T | O |
|---|---|
| 4 | 4 |
| – | 1 |
|   |   |

| T | O |
|---|---|
| 7 | 9 |
| – 6 | 9 |
|   |   |

| T | O |
|---|---|
| 7 | 3 |
| – 4 | 2 |
|   |   |

| T | O |
|---|---|
| 5 | 6 |
| – 2 | 3 |
|   |   |

| T | O |
|---|---|
| 9 | 9 |
| – | 0 |
|   |   |

| T | O |
|---|---|
| 6 | 3 |
| – 5 | 1 |
|   |   |

# Two-digit Subtraction

**Subtract.**

```
   8 6        2 7        7 2        1 6
 - 5 4      - 2 3      - 7 2      - 1 3
 -----      -----      -----      -----
   3 2
```

```
   5 9        7 5        6 3        9 4
 - 1 0      -   3      - 3 1      - 8 2
 -----      -----      -----      -----
```

```
   8 6        5 1        4 5        8 9
 - 2 2      - 5 0      - 1 5      - 6 0
 -----      -----      -----      -----
```

```
   6 9        3 8        1 4        8 9
 -   5      - 2 0      - 1 4      -   9
 -----      -----      -----      -----
```

```
   7 5        6 9        8 8        5 4
 - 2 3      - 4 0      -   7      - 2 2
 -----      -----      -----      -----
```

```
   1 6        4 8        7 4        5 0
 -   3      - 3 0      - 1 1      - 2 0
 -----      -----      -----      -----
```

# Two-digit Subtraction

Shade all the areas that have a difference of 21.

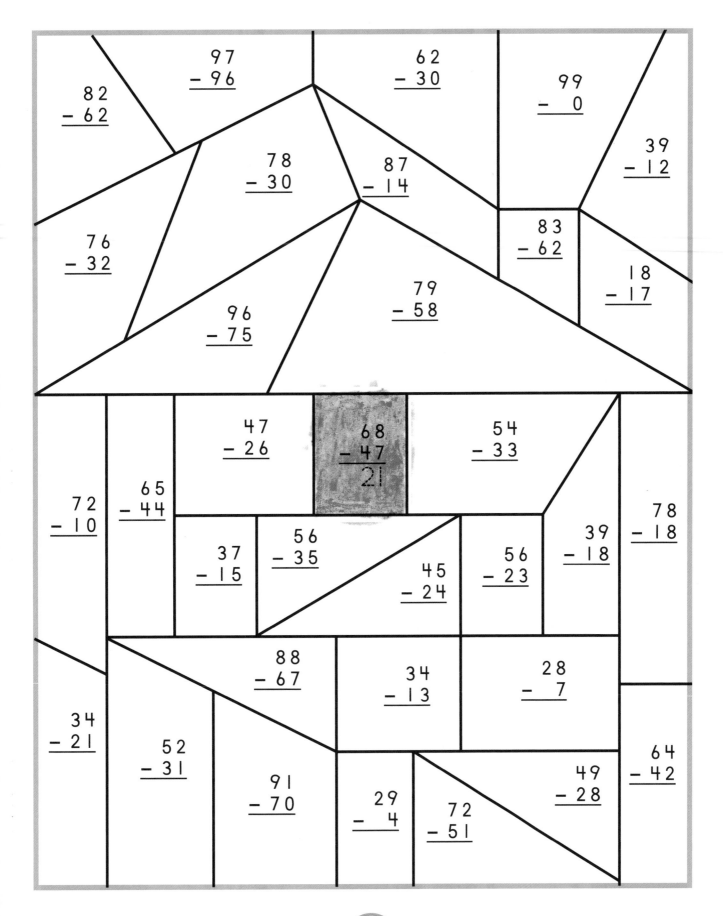

$$\begin{array}{r} 82 \\ -62 \\ \hline \end{array}$$

$$\begin{array}{r} 97 \\ -96 \\ \hline \end{array}$$

$$\begin{array}{r} 62 \\ -30 \\ \hline \end{array}$$

$$\begin{array}{r} 99 \\ -\ 0 \\ \hline \end{array}$$

$$\begin{array}{r} 39 \\ -12 \\ \hline \end{array}$$

$$\begin{array}{r} 78 \\ -30 \\ \hline \end{array}$$

$$\begin{array}{r} 87 \\ -14 \\ \hline \end{array}$$

$$\begin{array}{r} 76 \\ -32 \\ \hline \end{array}$$

$$\begin{array}{r} 83 \\ -62 \\ \hline \end{array}$$

$$\begin{array}{r} 18 \\ -17 \\ \hline \end{array}$$

$$\begin{array}{r} 96 \\ -75 \\ \hline \end{array}$$

$$\begin{array}{r} 79 \\ -58 \\ \hline \end{array}$$

$$\begin{array}{r} 47 \\ -26 \\ \hline \end{array}$$

$$\begin{array}{r} 68 \\ -47 \\ \hline 21 \end{array}$$

$$\begin{array}{r} 54 \\ -33 \\ \hline \end{array}$$

$$\begin{array}{r} 72 \\ -10 \\ \hline \end{array}$$

$$\begin{array}{r} 65 \\ -44 \\ \hline \end{array}$$

$$\begin{array}{r} 78 \\ -18 \\ \hline \end{array}$$

$$\begin{array}{r} 37 \\ -15 \\ \hline \end{array}$$

$$\begin{array}{r} 56 \\ -35 \\ \hline \end{array}$$

$$\begin{array}{r} 45 \\ -24 \\ \hline \end{array}$$

$$\begin{array}{r} 56 \\ -23 \\ \hline \end{array}$$

$$\begin{array}{r} 39 \\ -18 \\ \hline \end{array}$$

$$\begin{array}{r} 88 \\ -67 \\ \hline \end{array}$$

$$\begin{array}{r} 34 \\ -13 \\ \hline \end{array}$$

$$\begin{array}{r} 28 \\ -\ 7 \\ \hline \end{array}$$

$$\begin{array}{r} 34 \\ -21 \\ \hline \end{array}$$

$$\begin{array}{r} 52 \\ -31 \\ \hline \end{array}$$

$$\begin{array}{r} 91 \\ -70 \\ \hline \end{array}$$

$$\begin{array}{r} 29 \\ -\ 4 \\ \hline \end{array}$$

$$\begin{array}{r} 72 \\ -51 \\ \hline \end{array}$$

$$\begin{array}{r} 49 \\ -28 \\ \hline \end{array}$$

$$\begin{array}{r} 64 \\ -42 \\ \hline \end{array}$$

# Three-digit Subtraction

Use these steps to subtract three-digit numbers.

**Find: 874 - 671**

| Step 1<br>Subtract the<br>ones.<br>(4 − 1 = 3) | Step 2<br>Subtract the<br>tens.<br>(7 − 7 = 0) | Step 3<br>Subtract the<br>hundreds.<br>(8 − 6 = 2) |
|---|---|---|
| H T O<br>8 7 4<br>− 6 7 1<br>‾‾‾‾ 3 | H T O<br>8 7 4<br>− 6 7 1<br>‾‾ 0 3 | H T O<br>8 7 4<br>− 6 7 1<br>2 0 3 |

**Subtract.**

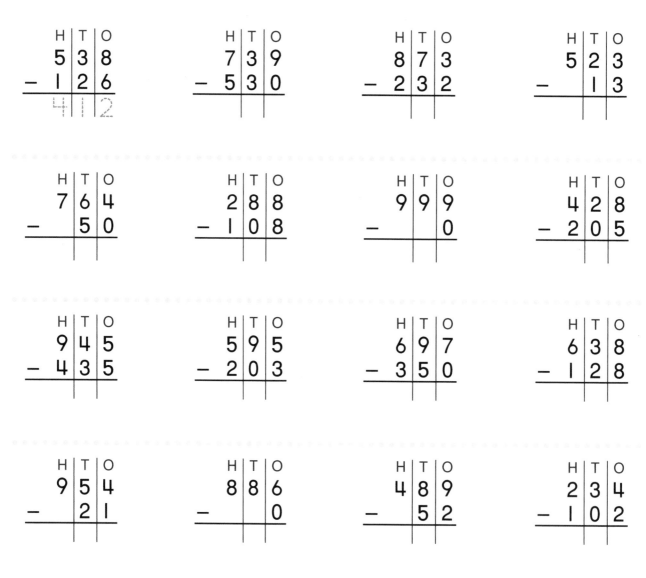

|   | H T O<br>5 3 8<br>− 1 2 6<br>4 1 2 | H T O<br>7 3 9<br>− 5 3 0 | H T O<br>8 7 3<br>− 2 3 2 | H T O<br>5 2 3<br>−   1 3 |
|---|---|---|---|---|
|   | H T O<br>7 6 4<br>−   5 0 | H T O<br>2 8 8<br>− 1 0 8 | H T O<br>9 9 9<br>−     0 | H T O<br>4 2 8<br>− 2 0 5 |
|   | H T O<br>9 4 5<br>− 4 3 5 | H T O<br>5 9 5<br>− 2 0 3 | H T O<br>6 9 7<br>− 3 5 0 | H T O<br>6 3 8<br>− 1 2 8 |
|   | H T O<br>9 5 4<br>−   2 1 | H T O<br>8 8 6<br>−     0 | H T O<br>4 8 9<br>−   5 2 | H T O<br>2 3 4<br>− 1 0 2 |

# Two-digit Subtraction with Regrouping

### Regroup the tens. Cross out ones to subtract.

23
− 8
15

2 tens    3 ones  =  ___1___ ten  ___13___ ones

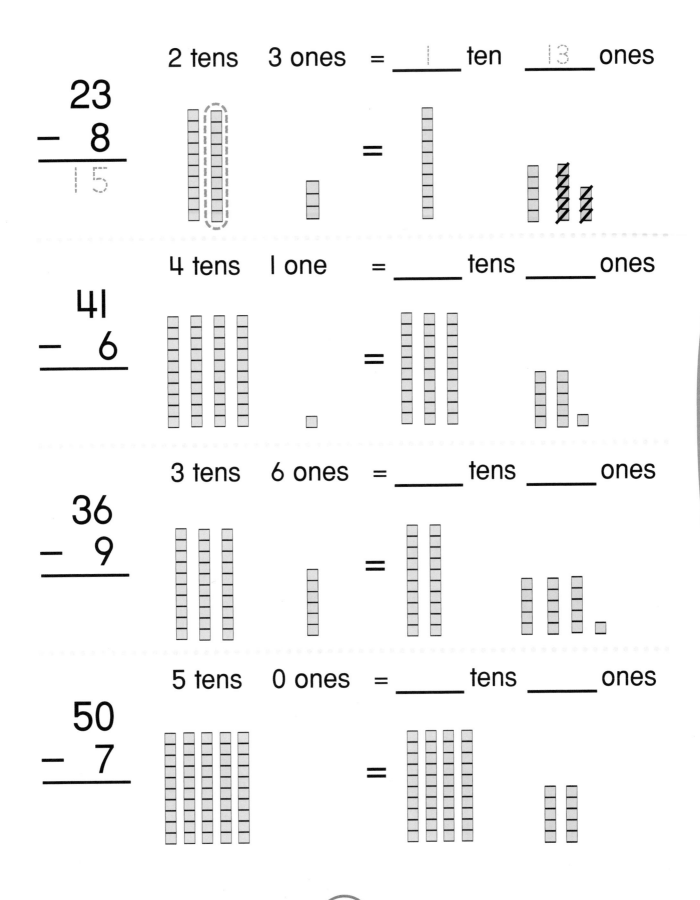

41
− 6

4 tens    1 one   =  _____ tens _____ ones

36
− 9

3 tens    6 ones  =  _____ tens _____ ones

50
− 7

5 tens    0 ones  =  _____ tens _____ ones

# Two-digit Subtraction with Regrouping

Regroup the tens. Cross out tens and ones to subtract.

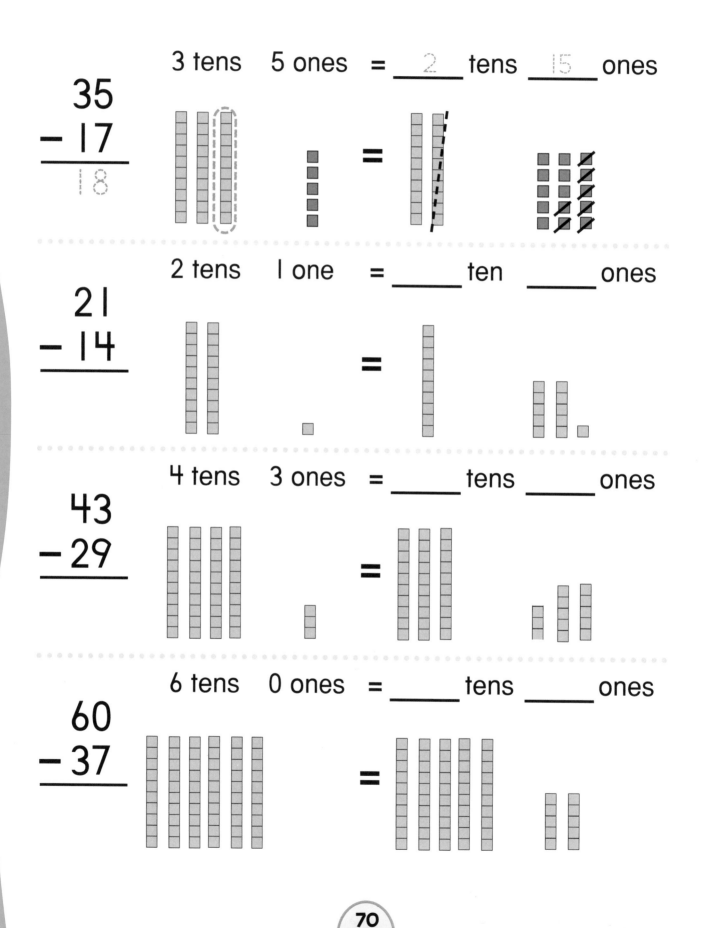

3 tens   5 ones   = ___2___ tens ___15___ ones

$$\begin{array}{r} 35 \\ -\ 17 \\ \hline 18 \end{array}$$

2 tens   1 one   = _____ ten _____ ones

$$\begin{array}{r} 21 \\ -\ 14 \\ \hline \end{array}$$

4 tens   3 ones   = _____ tens _____ ones

$$\begin{array}{r} 43 \\ -29 \\ \hline \end{array}$$

6 tens   0 ones   = _____ tens _____ ones

$$\begin{array}{r} 60 \\ -37 \\ \hline \end{array}$$

# Two-digit Subtraction with Regrouping

Use these steps to subtract two-digit numbers with regrouping.

**Find: 52- 13**

| Step 1 | Step 2 | Step 3 | Step 4 |
|--------|--------|--------|--------|
| Subtract ones. More ones are needed. (2 − 3 = ?) | Regroup. Show 1 less ten and 10 more ones. | Subtract the ones. (12 − 3 = 9) | Subtract the tens. (4 − 1 = 3) |

Step 1:
```
   T | O
   5 | 2
 − 1 | 3
   ___
     ?
```

Step 2:
```
  4 |12
   T | O
   5̷ | 2̷
 − 1 | 3
```

Step 3:
```
  4 |12
   T | O
   5̷ | 2̷
 − 1 | 3
   ___
     9
```

Step 4:
```
  4 |12
   T | O
   5̷ | 2̷
 − 1 | 3
   ___
   3 | 9
```

**Subtract.**

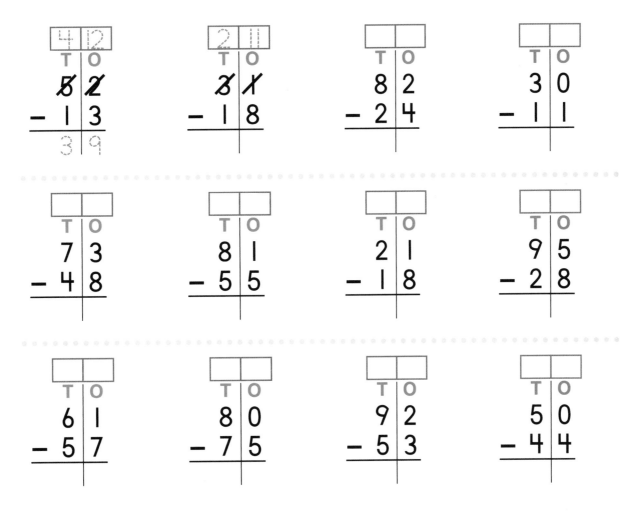

```
  4 12          2 11
   T | O          T | O          T | O          T | O
   5̷ | 2̷          5̷ | 1̷          8 | 2          3 | 0
 − 1 | 3        − 1 | 8        − 2 | 4        − 1 | 1
   ___
   3 | 9
```

```
   T | O          T | O          T | O          T | O
   7 | 3          8 | 1          2 | 1          9 | 5
 − 4 | 8        − 5 | 5        − 1 | 8        − 2 | 8
```

```
   T | O          T | O          T | O          T | O
   6 | 1          8 | 0          9 | 2          5 | 0
 − 5 | 7        − 7 | 5        − 5 | 3        − 4 | 4
```

# Two-digit Subtraction with Regrouping

Subtract.

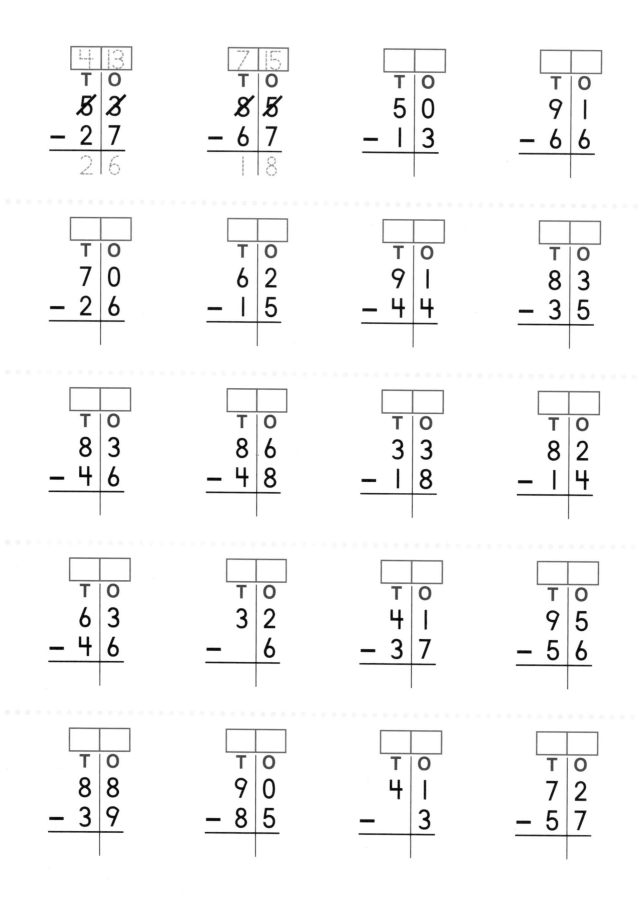

| | | |
|---|---|---|
| 4 13 | 7 15 | |

**T O**
8̸ 3̸
− 2 7
2 6

**T O**
8̸ 5̸
− 6 7
1 8

**T O**
5 0
− 1 3

**T O**
9 1
− 6 6

**T O**
7 0
− 2 6

**T O**
6 2
− 1 5

**T O**
9 1
− 4 4

**T O**
8 3
− 3 5

**T O**
8 3
− 4 6

**T O**
8 6
− 4 8

**T O**
3 3
− 1 8

**T O**
8 2
− 1 4

**T O**
6 3
− 4 6

**T O**
3 2
−   6

**T O**
4 1
− 3 7

**T O**
9 5
− 5 6

**T O**
8 8
− 3 9

**T O**
9 0
− 8 5

**T O**
4 1
−   3

**T O**
7 2
− 5 7

**Match the equal differences.**

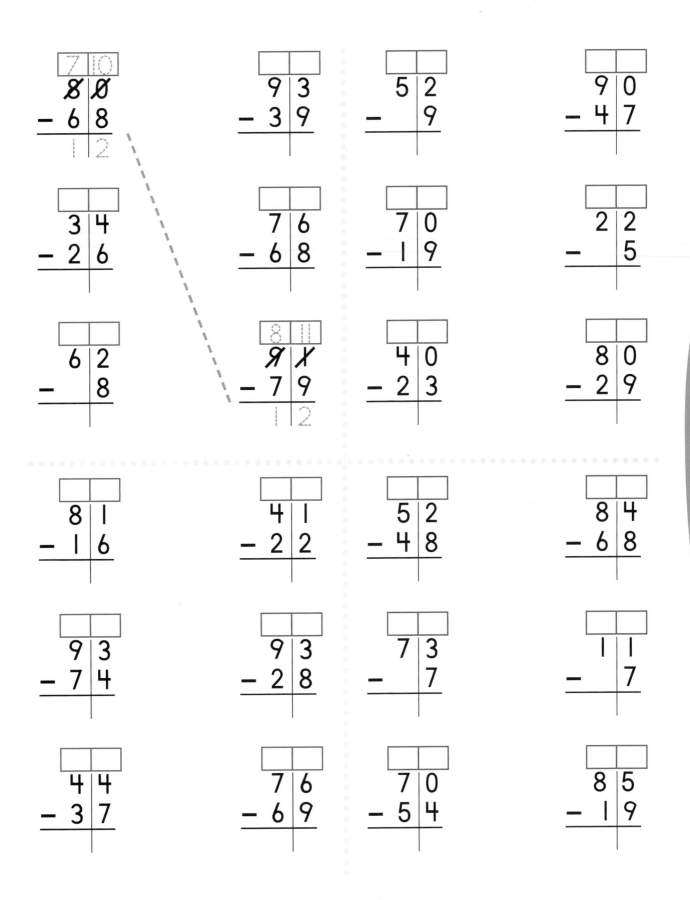

# Two-digit Subtraction with Regrouping

Subtract.

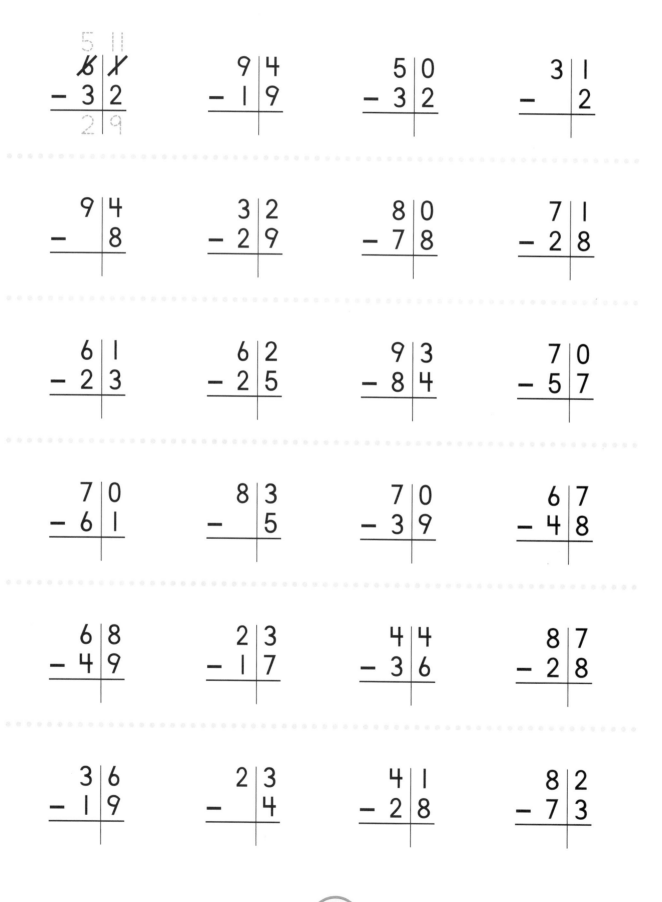

$$
\begin{array}{r}
5\ \ 11\\
\not{6}\ \not{1}\\
-\ 3\ 2\\
\hline
2\ 9
\end{array}
\qquad
\begin{array}{r}
9\ 4\\
-\ 1\ 9\\
\hline
\end{array}
\qquad
\begin{array}{r}
5\ 0\\
-\ 3\ 2\\
\hline
\end{array}
\qquad
\begin{array}{r}
3\ 1\\
-\ \ \ 2\\
\hline
\end{array}
$$

$$
\begin{array}{r}
9\ 4\\
-\ \ \ 8\\
\hline
\end{array}
\qquad
\begin{array}{r}
3\ 2\\
-\ 2\ 9\\
\hline
\end{array}
\qquad
\begin{array}{r}
8\ 0\\
-\ 7\ 8\\
\hline
\end{array}
\qquad
\begin{array}{r}
7\ 1\\
-\ 2\ 8\\
\hline
\end{array}
$$

$$
\begin{array}{r}
6\ 1\\
-\ 2\ 3\\
\hline
\end{array}
\qquad
\begin{array}{r}
6\ 2\\
-\ 2\ 5\\
\hline
\end{array}
\qquad
\begin{array}{r}
9\ 3\\
-\ 8\ 4\\
\hline
\end{array}
\qquad
\begin{array}{r}
7\ 0\\
-\ 5\ 7\\
\hline
\end{array}
$$

$$
\begin{array}{r}
7\ 0\\
-\ 6\ 1\\
\hline
\end{array}
\qquad
\begin{array}{r}
8\ 3\\
-\ \ \ 5\\
\hline
\end{array}
\qquad
\begin{array}{r}
7\ 0\\
-\ 3\ 9\\
\hline
\end{array}
\qquad
\begin{array}{r}
6\ 7\\
-\ 4\ 8\\
\hline
\end{array}
$$

$$
\begin{array}{r}
6\ 8\\
-\ 4\ 9\\
\hline
\end{array}
\qquad
\begin{array}{r}
2\ 3\\
-\ 1\ 7\\
\hline
\end{array}
\qquad
\begin{array}{r}
4\ 4\\
-\ 3\ 6\\
\hline
\end{array}
\qquad
\begin{array}{r}
8\ 7\\
-\ 2\ 8\\
\hline
\end{array}
$$

$$
\begin{array}{r}
3\ 6\\
-\ 1\ 9\\
\hline
\end{array}
\qquad
\begin{array}{r}
2\ 3\\
-\ \ \ 4\\
\hline
\end{array}
\qquad
\begin{array}{r}
4\ 1\\
-\ 2\ 8\\
\hline
\end{array}
\qquad
\begin{array}{r}
8\ 2\\
-\ 7\ 3\\
\hline
\end{array}
$$

Look at the pictures. Write + or −. Then write the sum or difference.

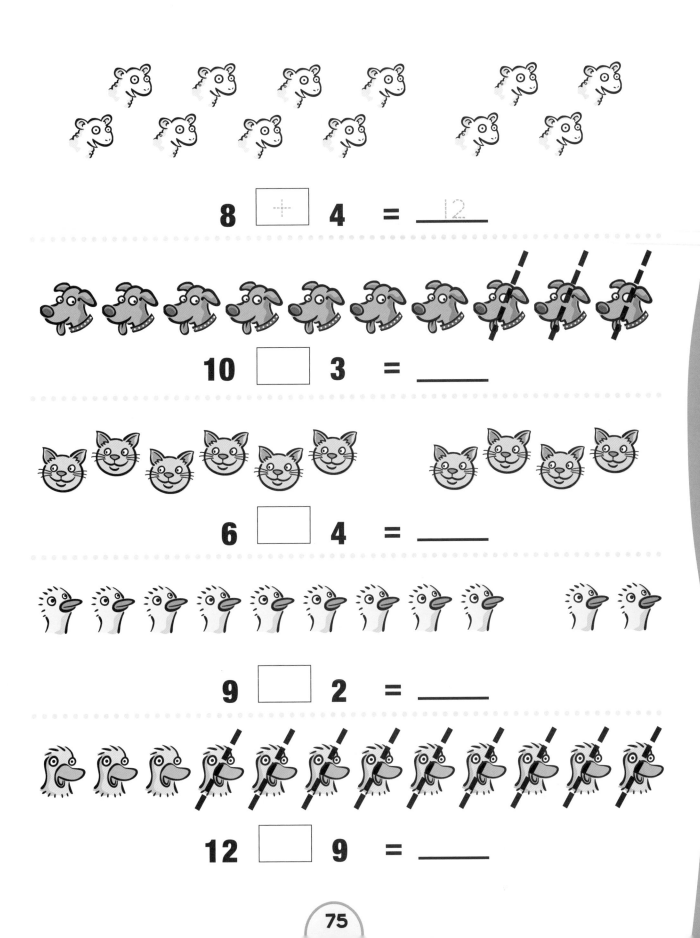

8 $\boxed{+}$ 4 = ___12___

10 $\boxed{\phantom{+}}$ 3 = _____

6 $\boxed{\phantom{+}}$ 4 = _____

9 $\boxed{\phantom{+}}$ 2 = _____

12 $\boxed{\phantom{+}}$ 9 = _____

**Subtract.**

$6 - 6 =$ _____          $14 - 5 =$ _____

$13 - 7 =$ _____          $8 - 0 =$ _____

**Complete the fact families.**

__5__ + __4__ = __9__          __7__ + __3__ = __10__

____ + ____ = ____          ____ + ____ = ____

____ − ____ = ____          ____ − ____ = ____

____ − ____ = ____          ____ − ____ = ____

**Subtract.**

```
   1 8          4 5          6 4          7 8
 −   3        − 2 3        − 5 1        − 5 1
```

```
   4 9 3        5 7 1        6 3 9        2 8 5
 − 1 6 3      − 1 4 0      − 3 0 5      − 2 1 4
```

```
   1 5          3 1          2 6          4 4
 −   6        − 2 5        − 1 8        − 3 9
```

```
   8 5          7 2
 − 5 6        − 3 8
```

**Write the number sentences to match the pictures.**

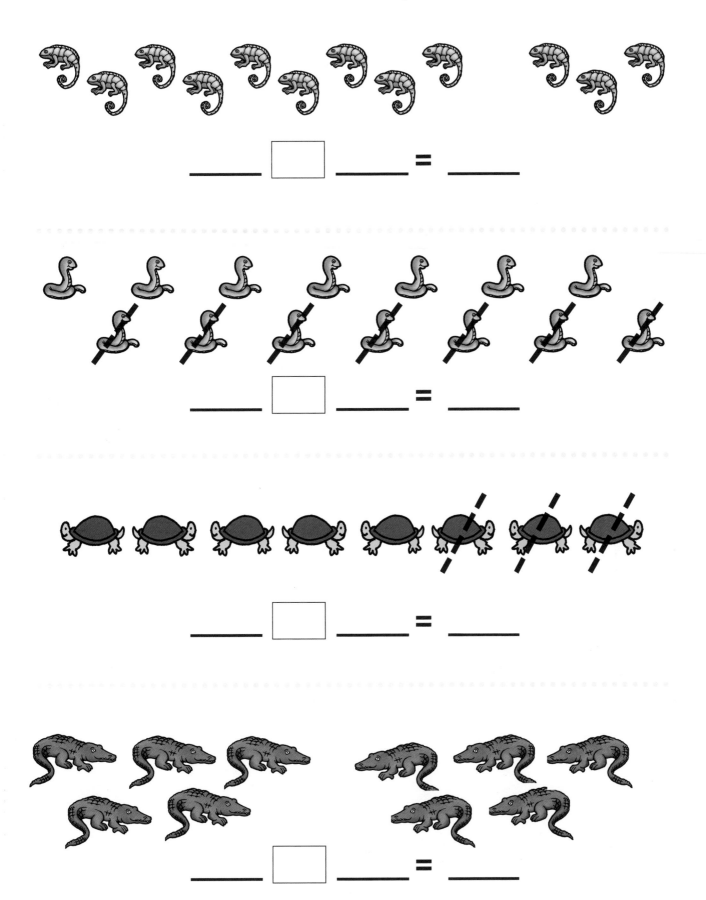

_____ [ ] _____ = _____

_____ [ ] _____ = _____

_____ [ ] _____ = _____

_____ [ ] _____ = _____

## Pennies

= I cent = I¢

**Count the money. Write the total amount on each bag.**

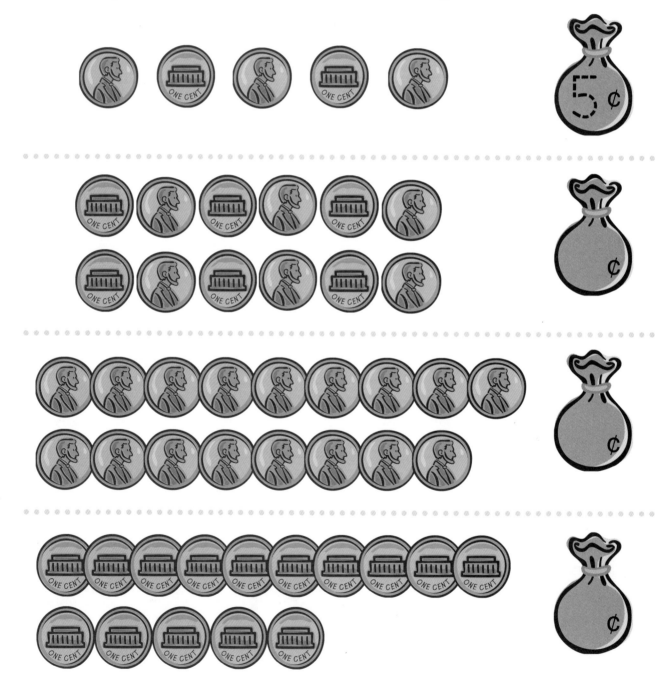

 = 5 cents = 5¢

Count the money. Write the total amount on each bag.

  8 ¢

  ___ ¢

  ___ ¢

  ___ ¢

  ___ ¢

# Pennies, Nickels, and Dimes

 = 10 cents = 10¢

Count the money. Write the total amount on each bag.

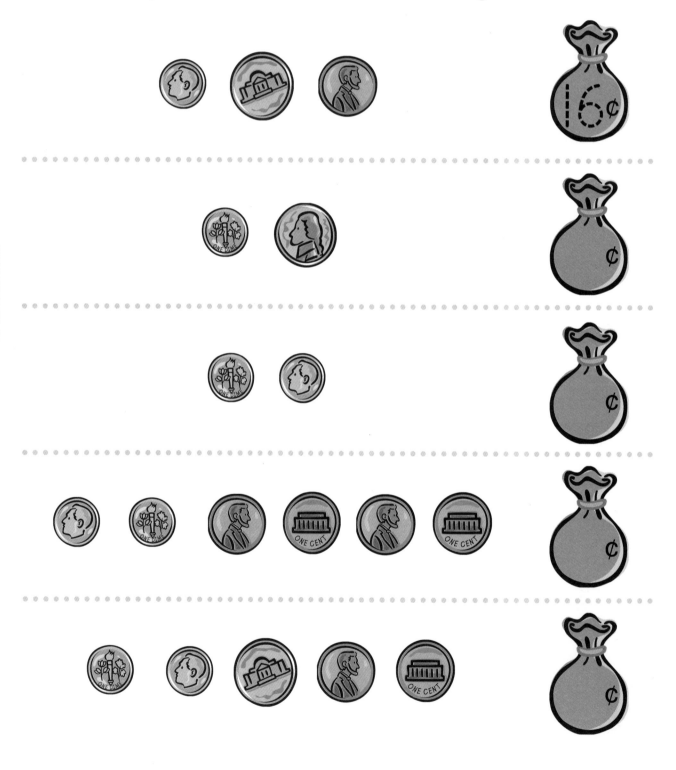

# Pennies, Nickels, and Dimes

Count the money. Circle the correct amount.

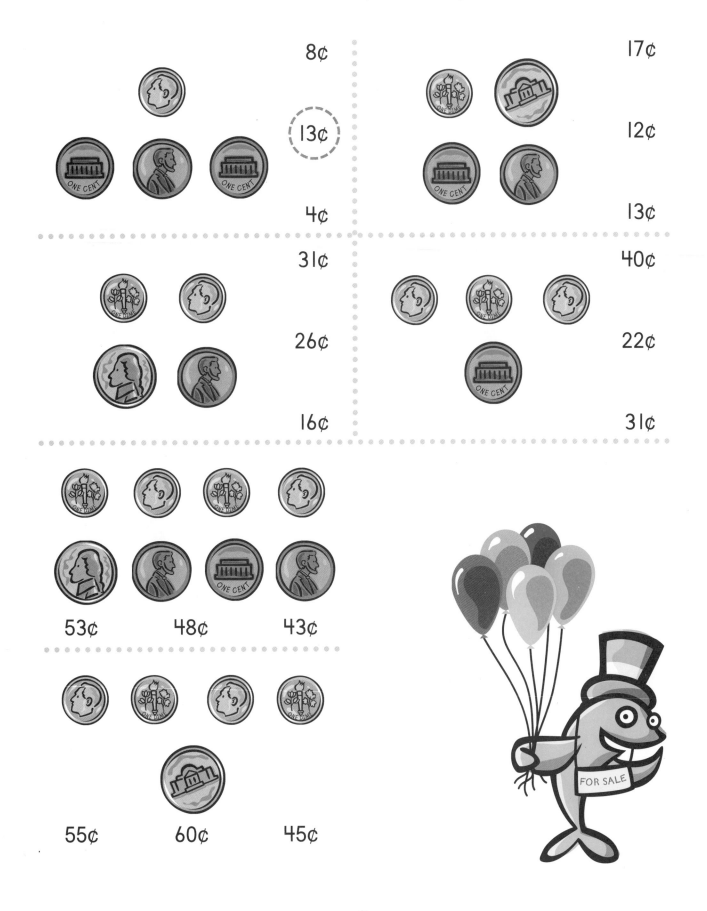

8¢

(13¢)

4¢

17¢

12¢

13¢

31¢

26¢

16¢

40¢

22¢

31¢

53¢     48¢     43¢

55¢     60¢     45¢

FOR SALE

# Pennies, Nickels, Dimes, and Quarters

 = 25 cents = 25¢

Count the money. Write the total amount on each bag.

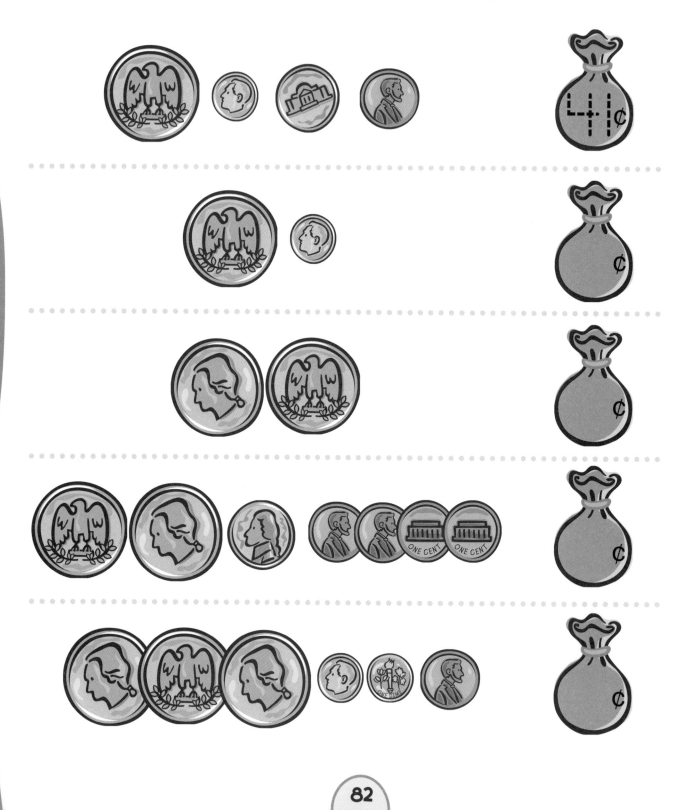

41¢

¢

¢

¢

¢

# Pennies, Nickels, Dimes, and Quarters

Match each item with the money that can buy it.

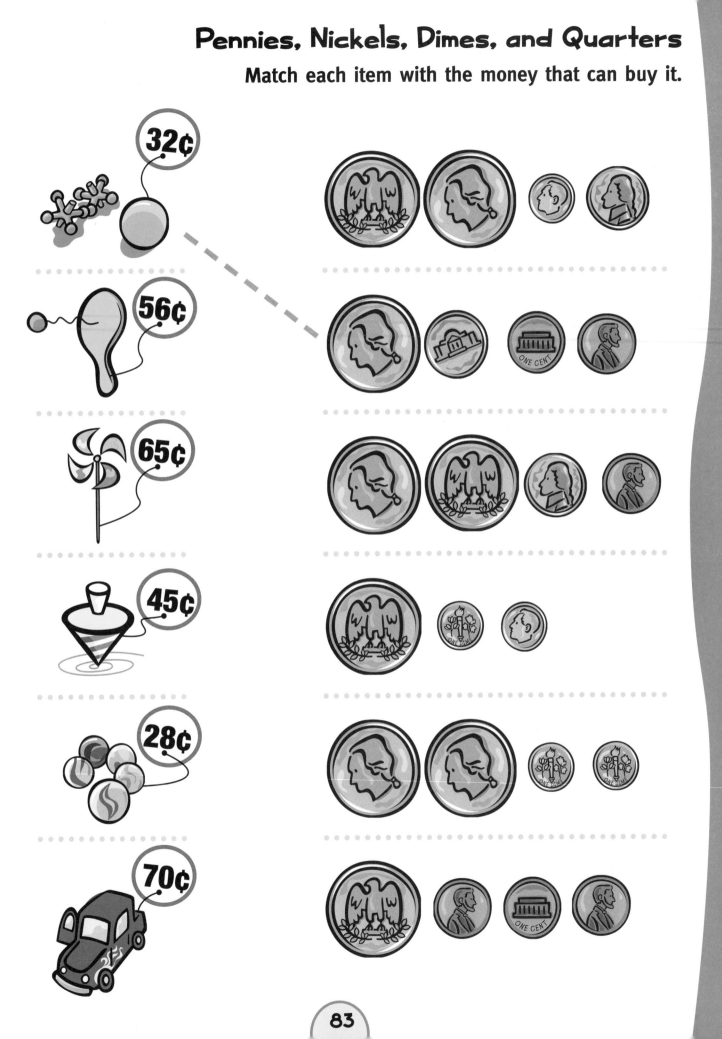

# Use Logic

Write two different ways to buy each item.

| | 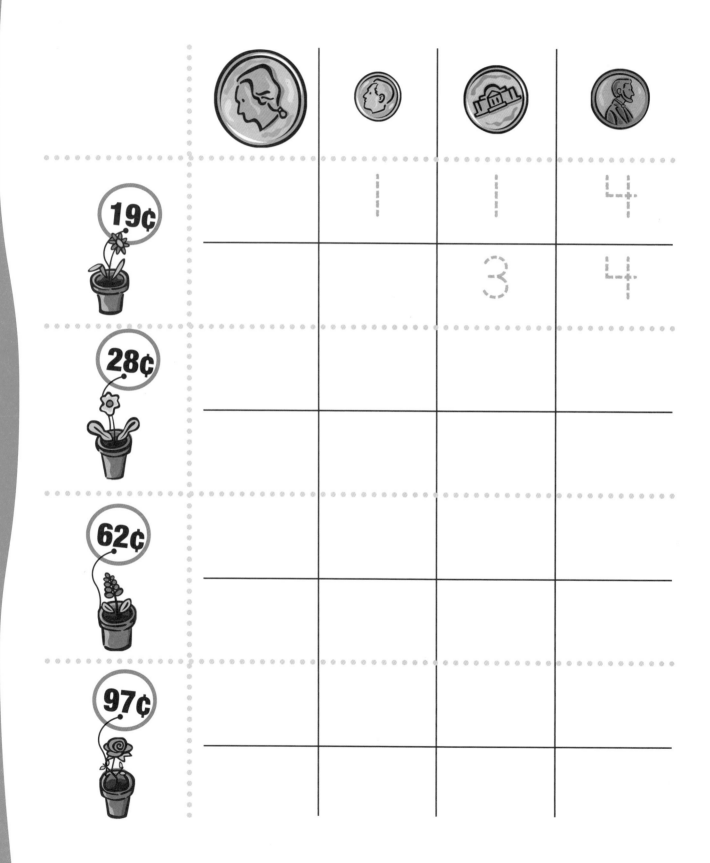 | | | |
|---|---|---|---|---|
| 19¢ | | 1 | 1 | 4 |
| | | | 3 | 4 |
| 28¢ | | | | |
| | | | | |
| 62¢ | | | | |
| | | | | |
| 97¢ | | | | |

# Money Equivalents

Match equal amounts of money.

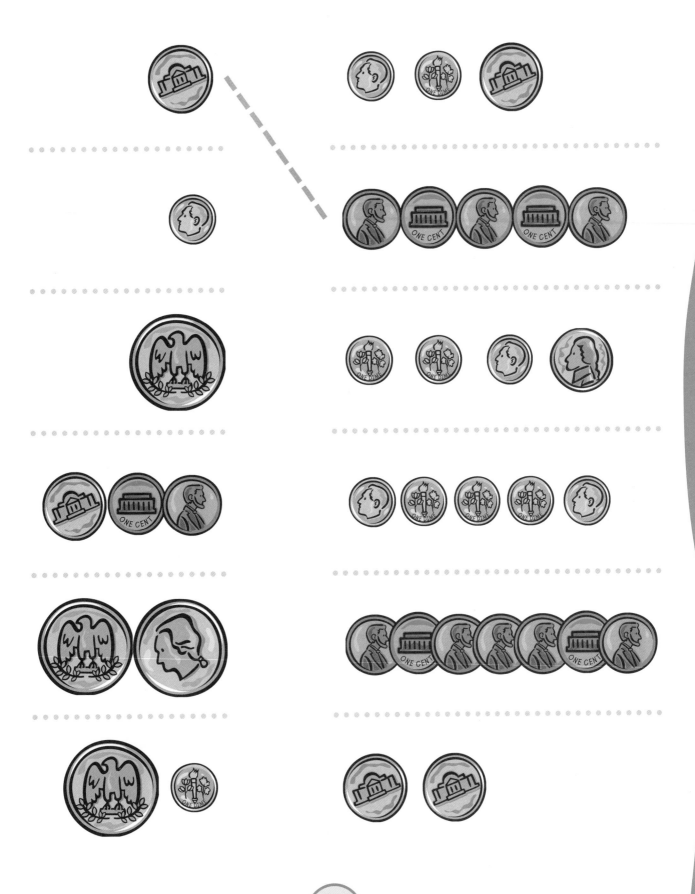

# Money Equivalents

Write how many of each coin you need to make the amount shown.

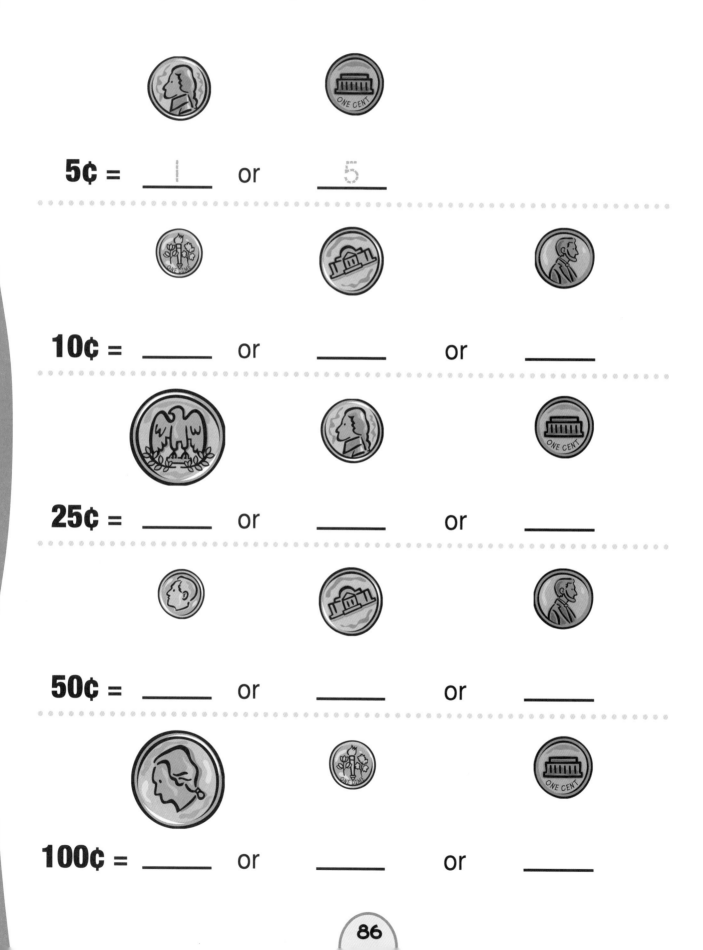

5¢ = __1__ or __5__

10¢ = _____ or _____ or _____

25¢ = _____ or _____ or _____

50¢ = _____ or _____ or _____

100¢ = _____ or _____ or _____

Circle the coins you need to buy each item.

35¢

49¢

17¢

89¢

# Use the Fewest Coins

Write how much money. Then draw the same amount with the fewest coins.

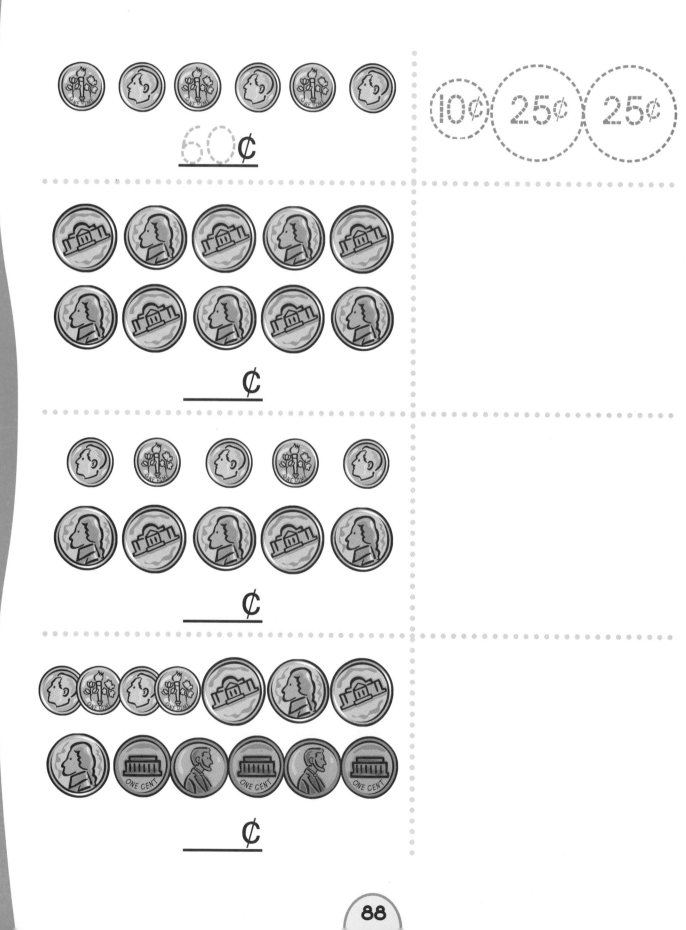

60 ¢

10¢  25¢  25¢

_____ ¢

_____ ¢

_____ ¢

88

# Making Change

Write how much change you get back.

| Price | You Pay | Your Change |
|:---:|:---:|:---:|

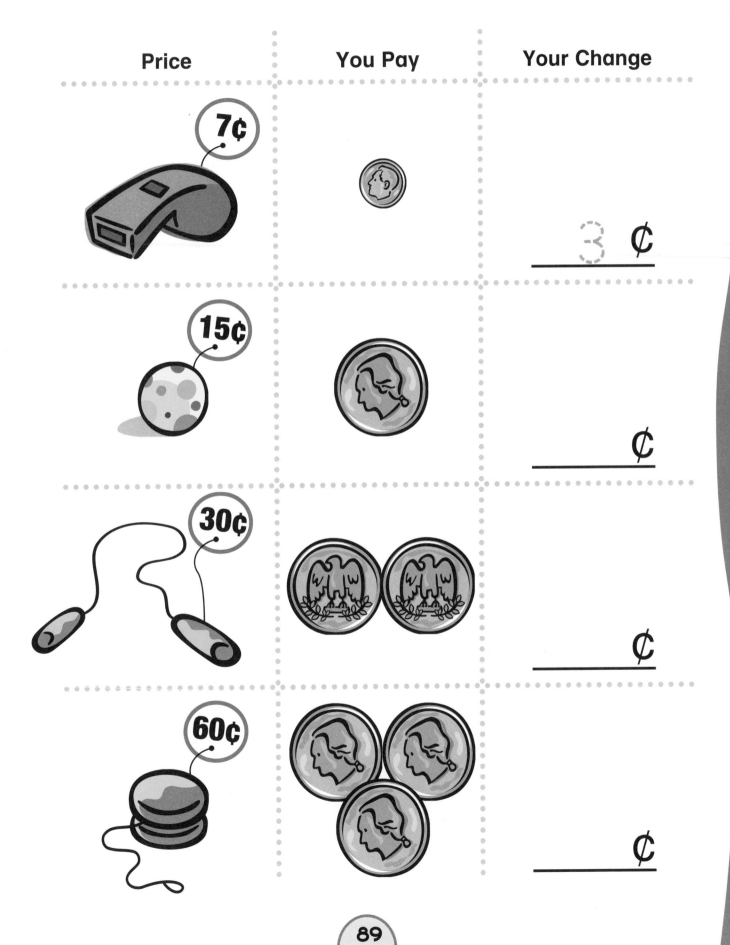

**7¢**       3 ¢

**15¢**       ___ ¢

**30¢**       ___ ¢

**60¢**       ___ ¢

# Making Change

Write how much change you get back.

| Price | You Pay | Your Change |
|---|---|---|
| 30¢ | | 20 ¢ |
| 27¢ | | ¢ |
| 58¢ | | ¢ |
| 17¢ | | ¢ |

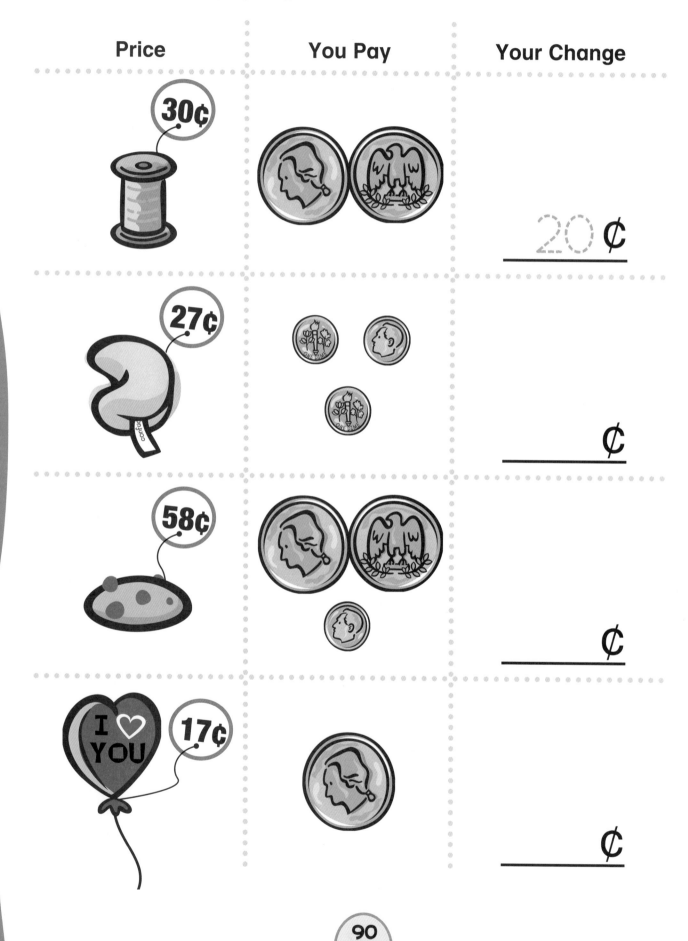

You pay 25¢ for each item. Write your change.

Apples
3¢ each

Pears
10¢ each

Pineapples
15¢ each

Peaches
5¢ each

Oranges
4¢ each

Bananas
20¢ each

You Pay: 25¢

22¢

You Pay: 25¢

_____ ¢

You Pay: 25¢

_____ ¢

You Pay: 25¢

_____ ¢

You Pay: 25¢

_____ ¢

You Pay: 25¢

_____ ¢

**Write how much money.**

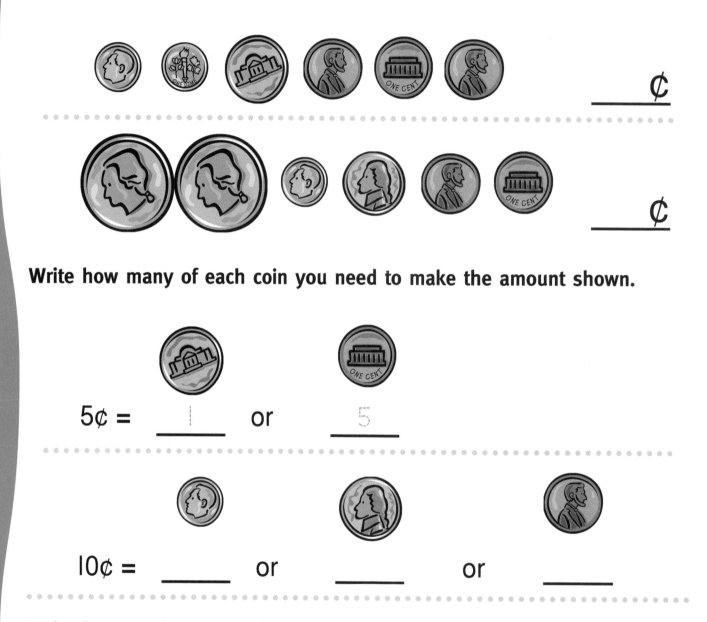

_____ ¢

_____ ¢

**Write how many of each coin you need to make the amount shown.**

5¢ = _____1_____ or _____5_____

10¢ = _____ or _____ or _____

**Write how much money. Then draw the same amount with the fewest coins.**

_____ ¢

**Write two different ways to buy each item.**

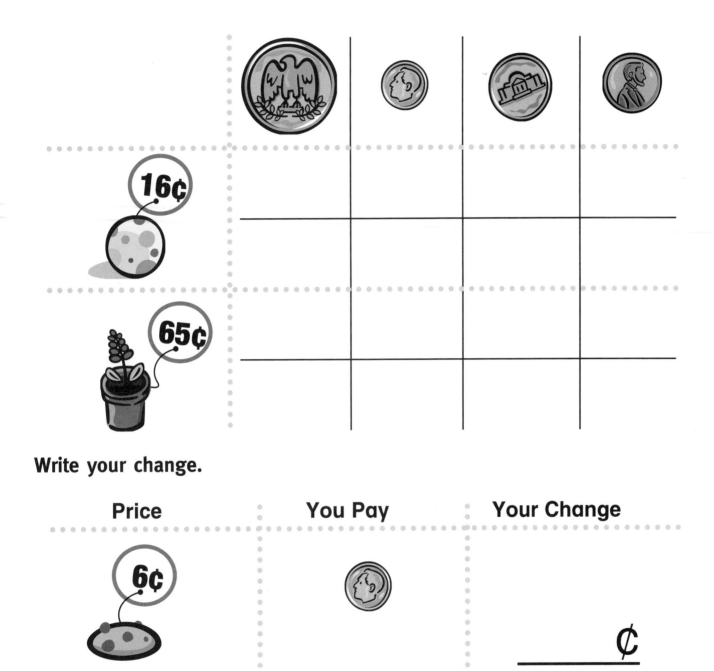

| | | | |
|---|---|---|---|
| **16¢** | | | |
| **65¢** | | | |

**Write your change.**

| Price | You Pay | Your Change |
|---|---|---|
| 6¢ |  | _____ ¢ |
| 17¢ | | _____ ¢ |

## Telling Time: Hours

Write the time shown on each clock in two ways.

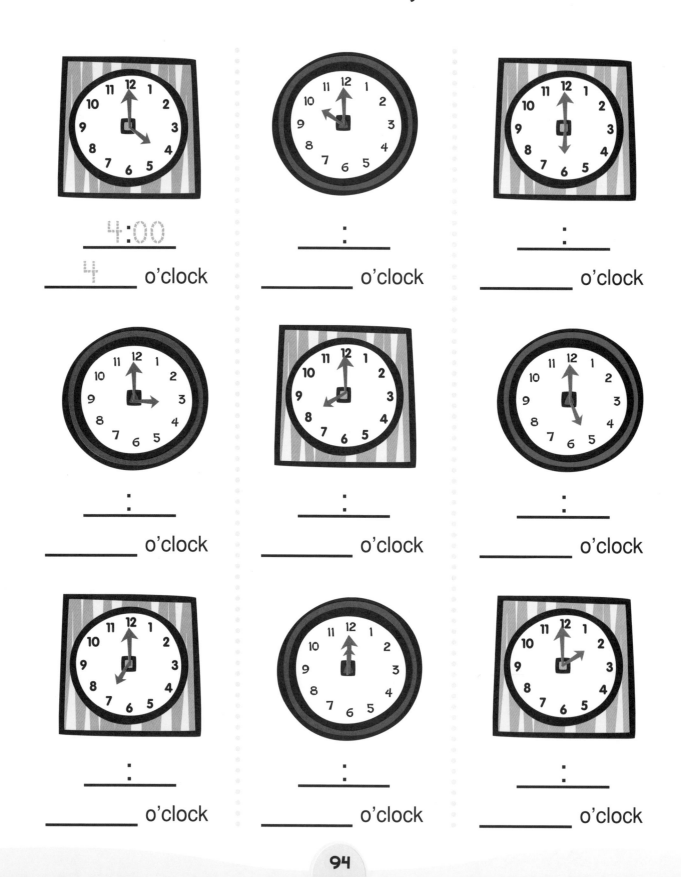

4:00

4 _____ o'clock

___:___

_____ o'clock

___:___

_____ o'clock

___:___

_____ o'clock

___:___

_____ o'clock

___:___

_____ o'clock

___:___

_____ o'clock

___:___

_____ o'clock

___:___

_____ o'clock

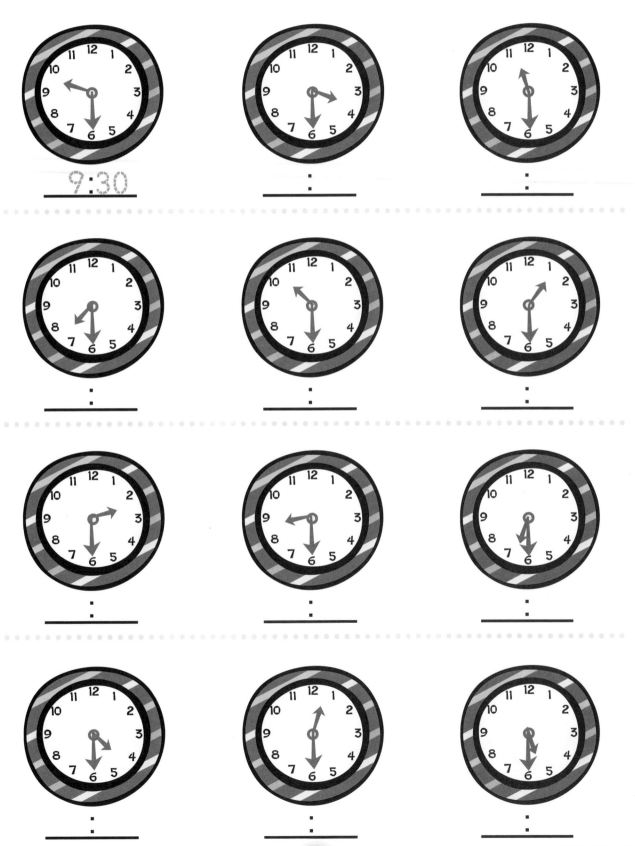

9:30

_____ : _____

_____ : _____

_____ : _____

_____ : _____

_____ : _____

_____ : _____

_____ : _____

_____ : _____

_____ : _____

_____ : _____

_____ : _____

# Telling Time: Quarter Hours

Write the time shown on each clock.

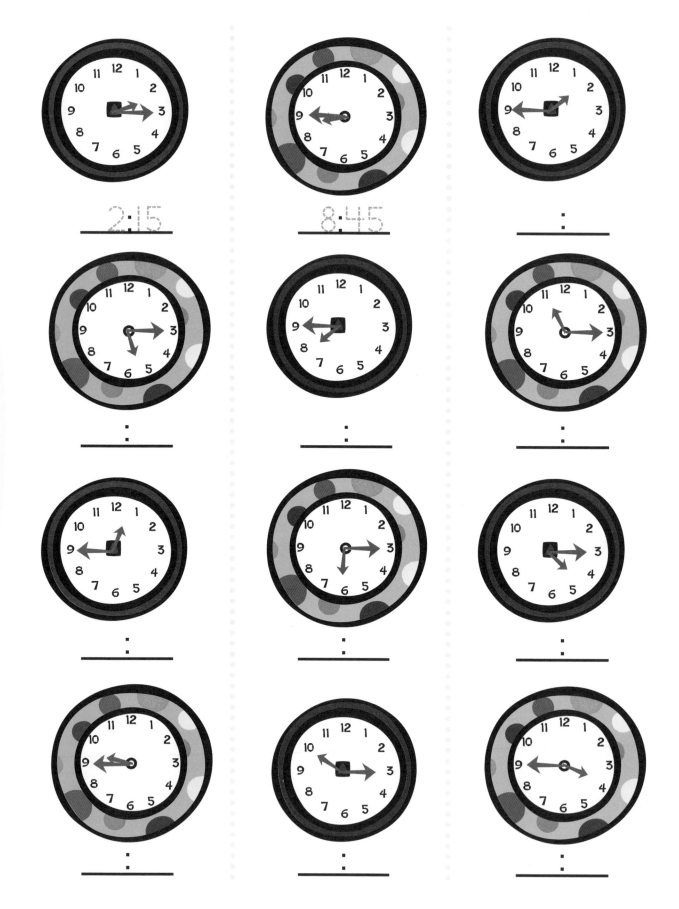

2:15

8:45

__:__

__:__

__:__

__:__

__:__

__:__

__:__

__:__

__:__

__:__

## Write the times that are a quarter hour later.

# Complete a Pattern

Draw the next clock in each pattern.

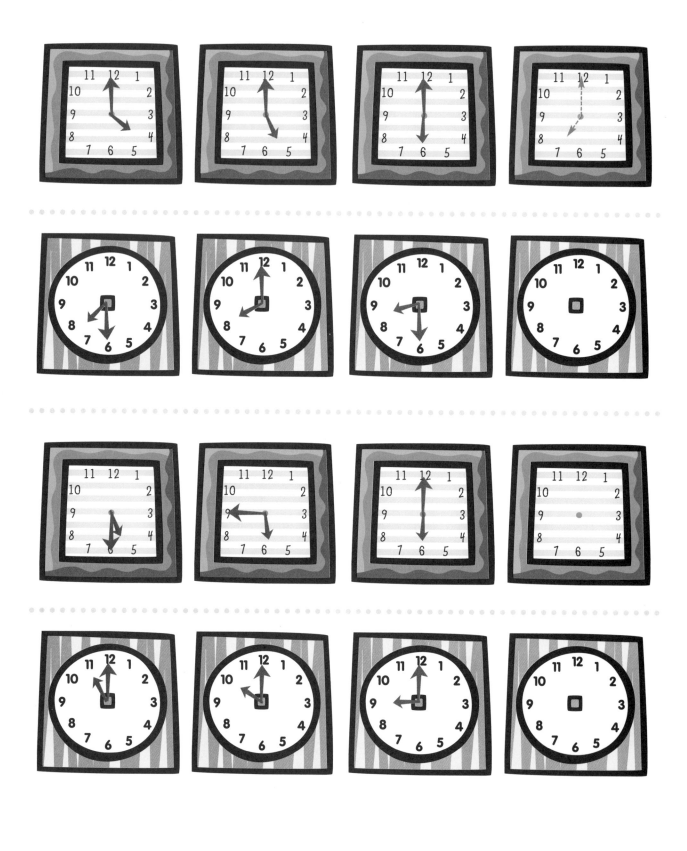

Write the time shown on each clock in two ways.

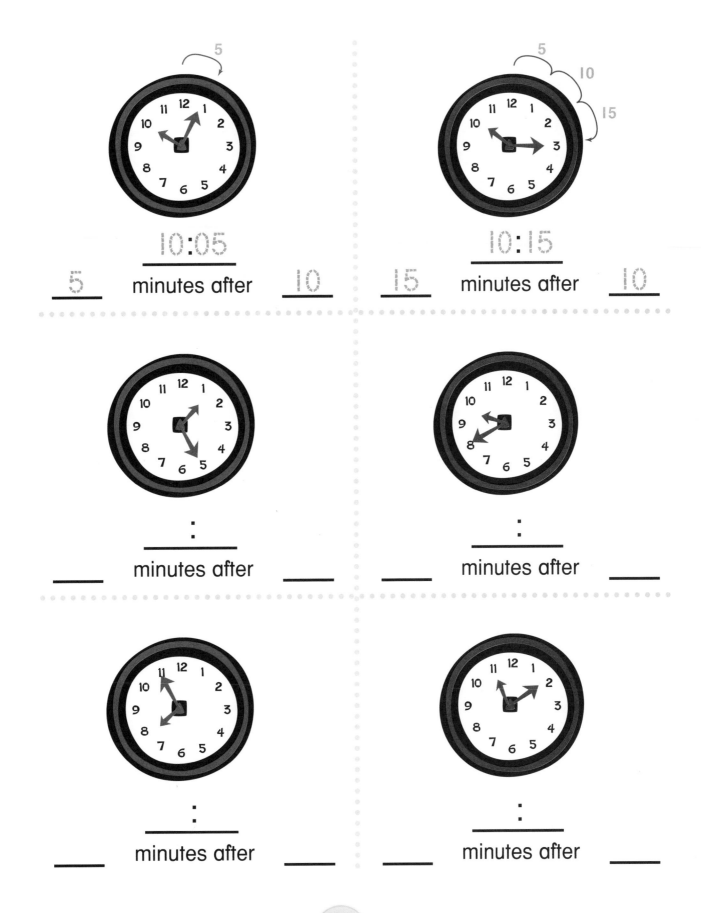

10:05

5 minutes after 10

10:15

15 minutes after 10

_:_

___ minutes after ___

_:_

___ minutes after ___

_:_

___ minutes after ___

_:_

___ minutes after ___

# Telling Time: Five Minutes

Write the times 5 minutes later.

# Practice Telling Time

## Match the clocks that show the same time.

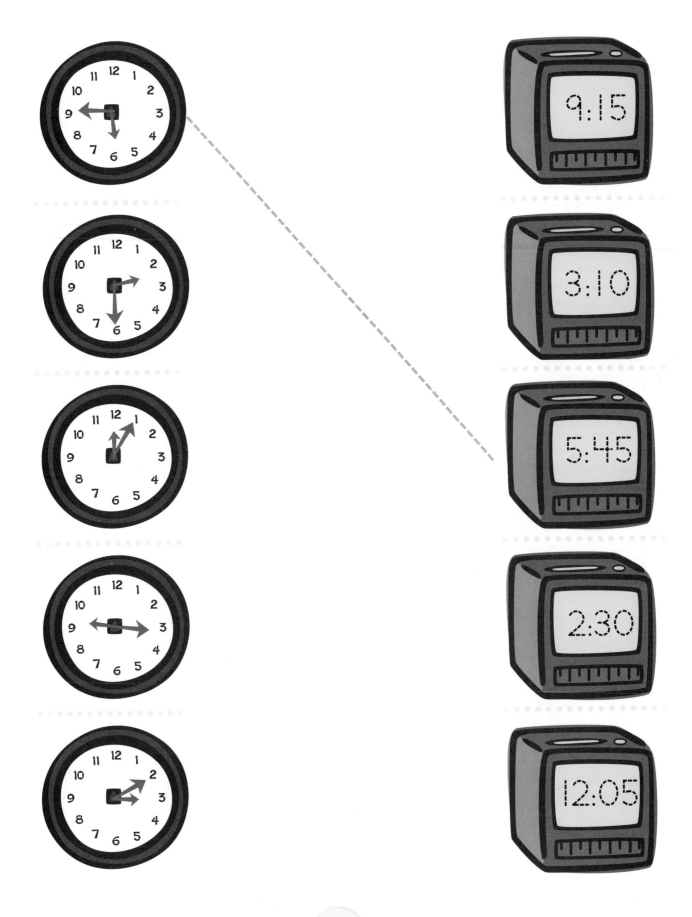

# Practice Telling Time

**Draw the hands on the clocks.**

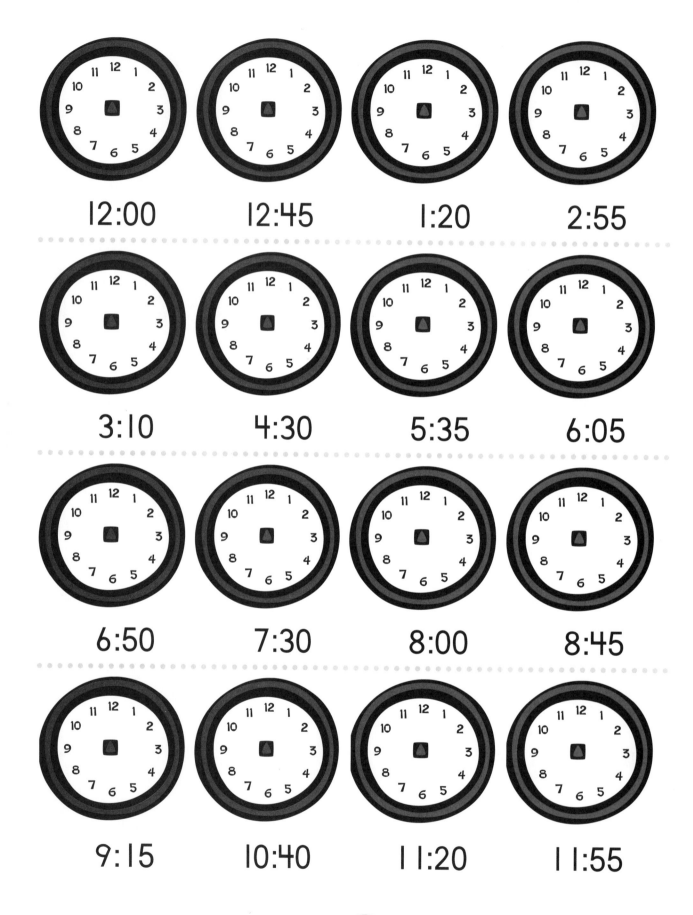

12:00     12:45     1:20     2:55

3:10     4:30     5:35     6:05

6:50     7:30     8:00     8:45

9:15     10:40     11:20     11:55

# Use Logic

## For each row, order the times.

# Write the time shown on each clock.

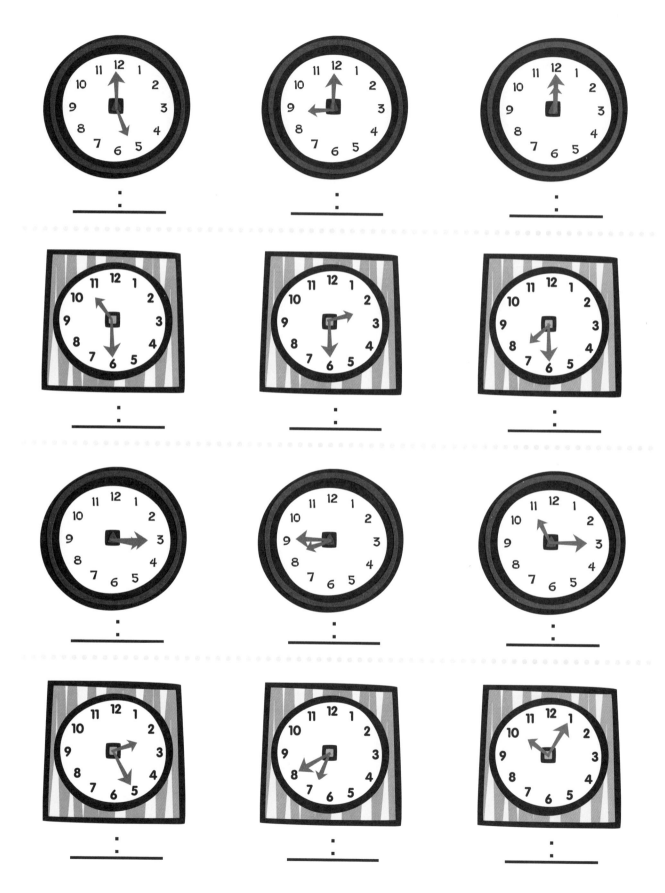

**Draw the next clock in each pattern.**

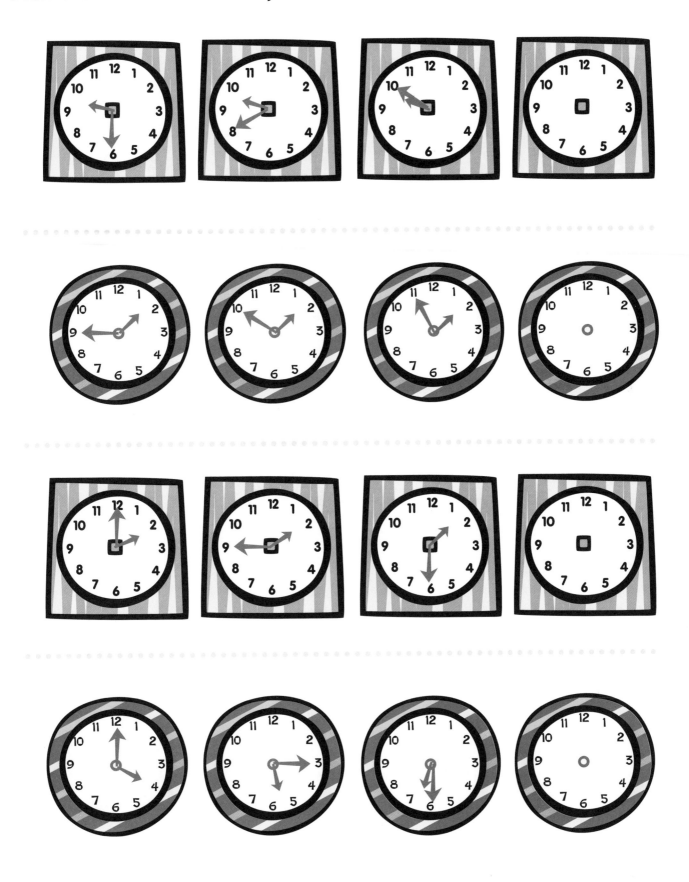

## Solid Figures

Circle the solids that are the same as the first figure in each row.

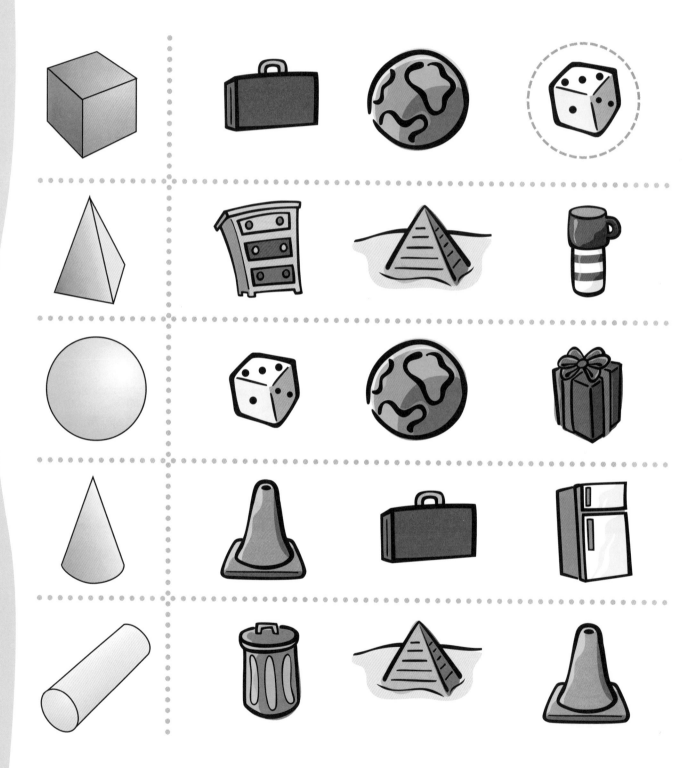

# Plane Figures

Circle the figures that are the same as the first figure in each row.

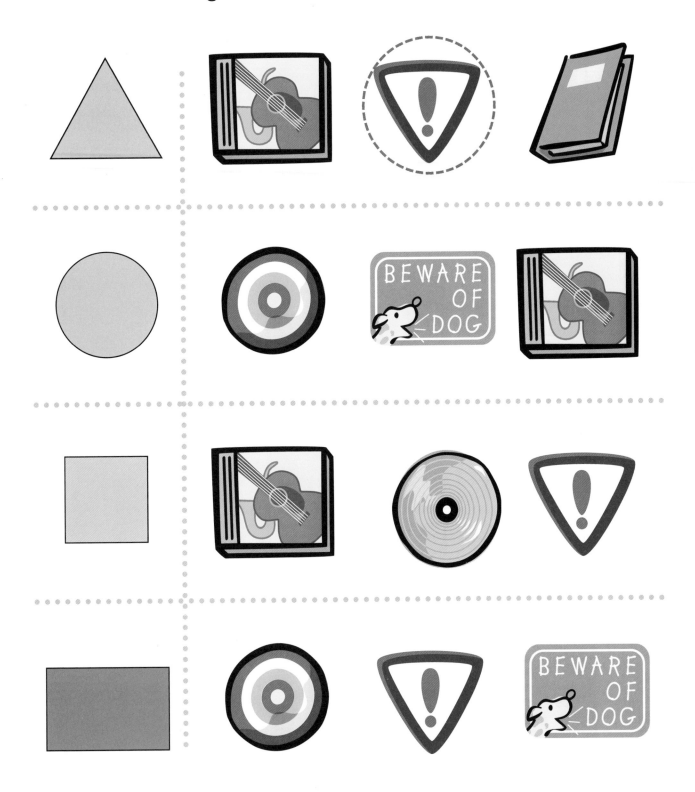

# Plane Figures

Name the figure. Then count its straight sides.

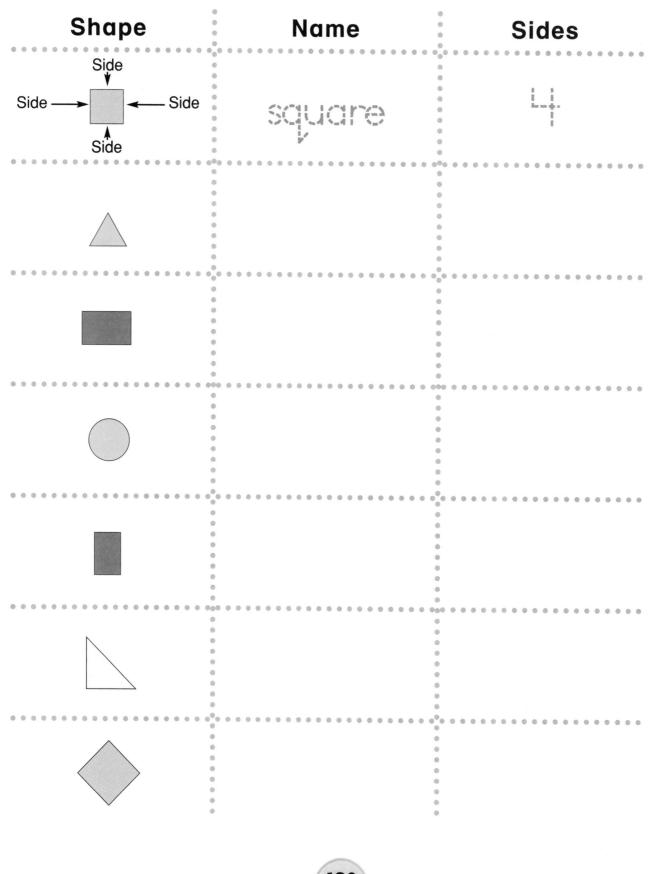

| Shape | Name | Sides |
|-------|------|-------|
| Side → ☐ ← Side (Side above, Side below) | square | 4 |
| △ | | |
| ▭ | | |
| ○ | | |
| ▯ | | |
| ◺ | | |
| ◇ | | |

# Congruence

Draw a figure to match each one shown.

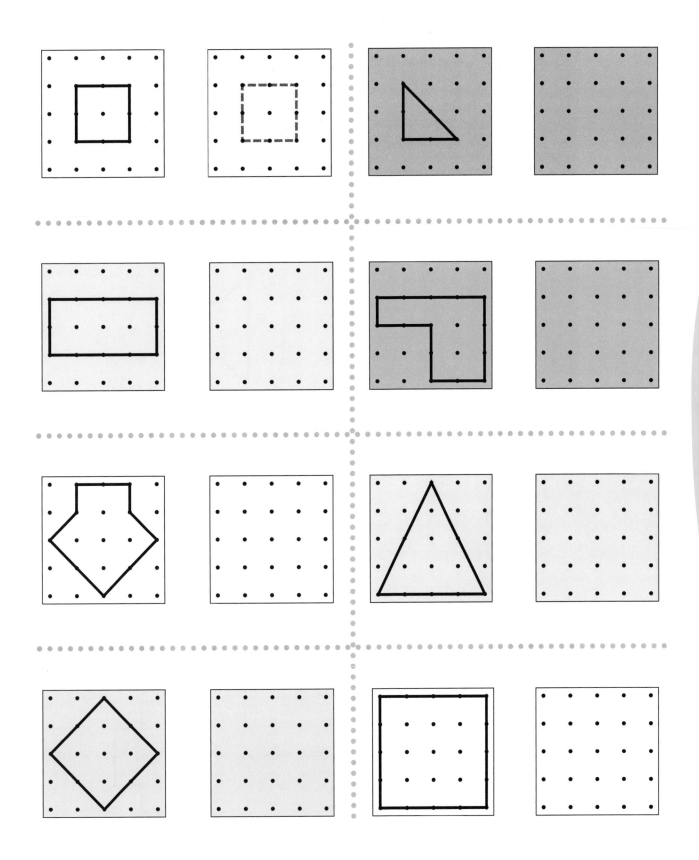

# Symmetry

Draw the other half of each figure.

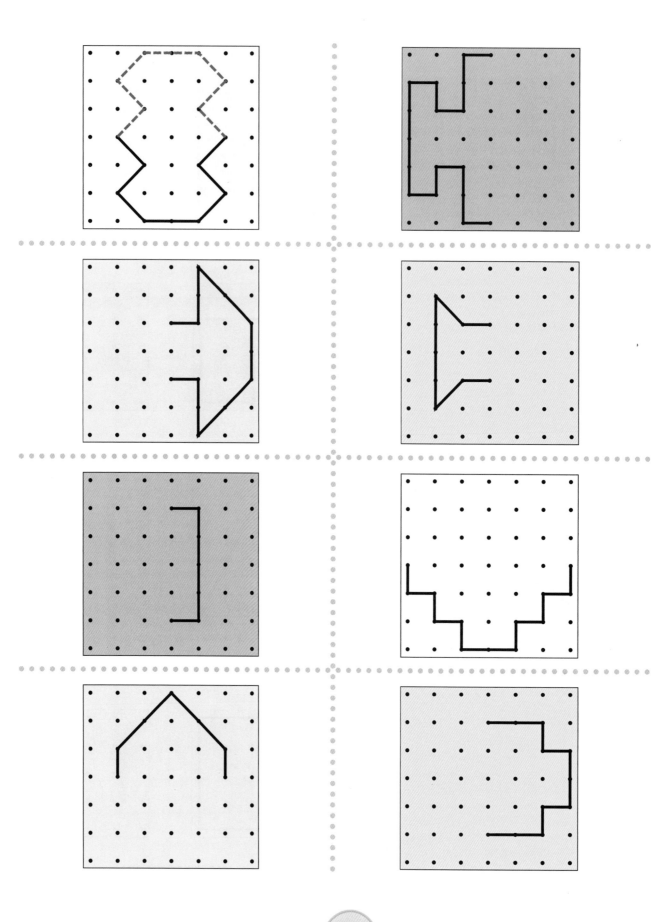

# Exploring Perimeter

## Count the number of units around each figure.

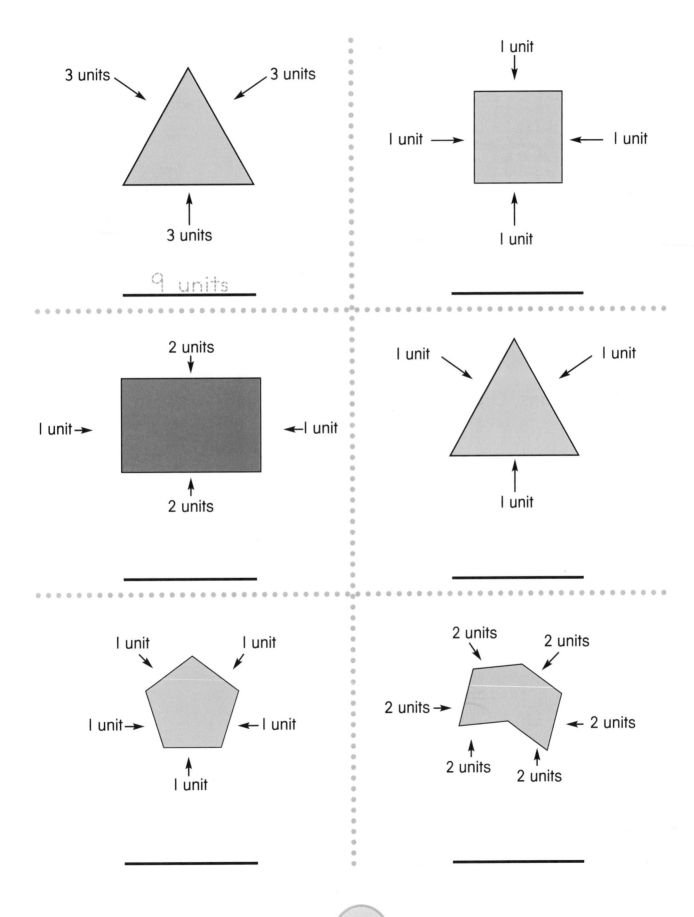

3 units     3 units

3 units

_9 units_

1 unit

1 unit     1 unit

1 unit

_____

2 units

1 unit     1 unit

2 units

_____

1 unit     1 unit

1 unit

_____

1 unit     1 unit

1 unit→     ←1 unit

1 unit

_____

2 units     2 units

2 units →     ← 2 units

2 units     2 units

_____

111

# Use a Picture

To find places on a grid,
always start at 0.
Count across ———→ .
Then count up ↑ .

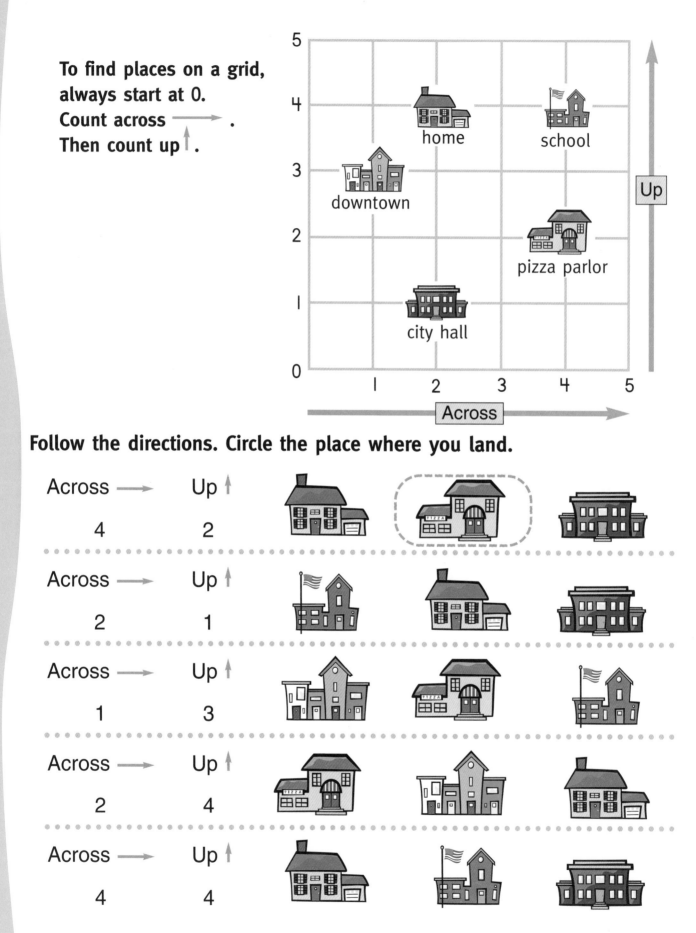

Follow the directions. Circle the place where you land.

| Across ——→ | Up ↑ | | | |
|---|---|---|---|---|
| 4 | 2 | | | |

| Across ——→ | Up ↑ | | | |
|---|---|---|---|---|
| 2 | 1 | | | |

| Across ——→ | Up ↑ | | | |
|---|---|---|---|---|
| 1 | 3 | | | |

| Across ——→ | Up ↑ | | | |
|---|---|---|---|---|
| 2 | 4 | | | |

| Across ——→ | Up ↑ | | | |
|---|---|---|---|---|
| 4 | 4 | | | |

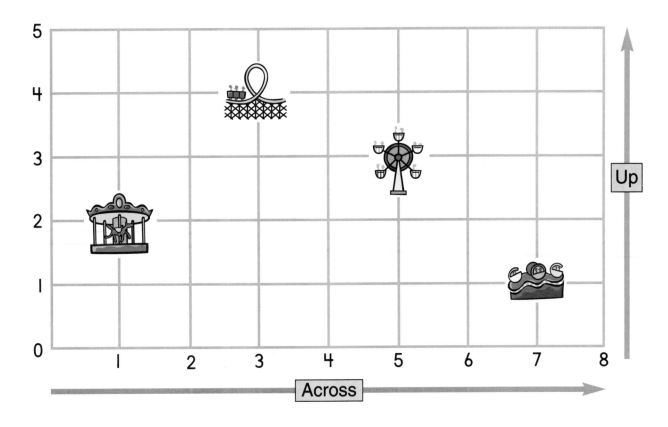

## Write the directions to each place.

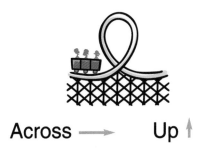

Across →    Up ↑

_____ 5      _____ 3

Across →    Up ↑

_____      _____

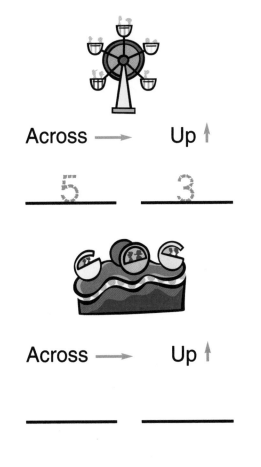

Across →    Up ↑

_____      _____

Across →    Up ↑

_____      _____

**Circle the shapes that are the same in each row.**

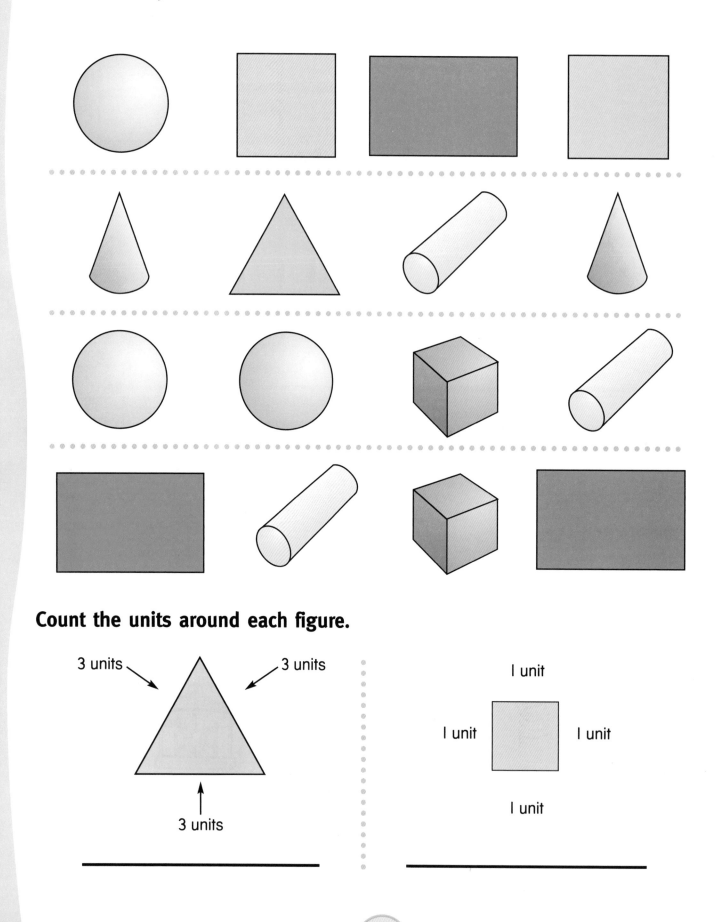

**Count the units around each figure.**

3 units     3 units

3 units

I unit

I unit     I unit

I unit

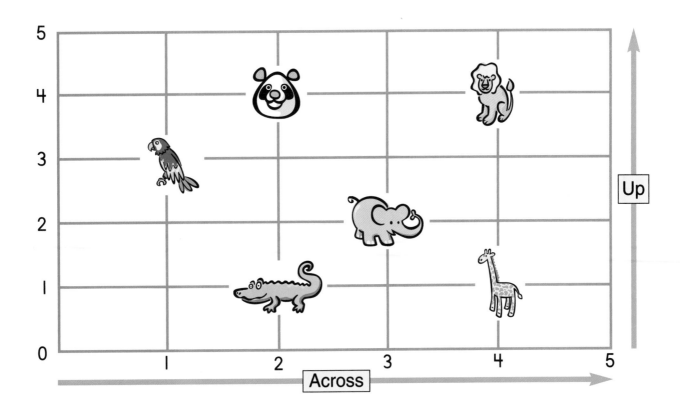

**Follow the directions. Circle the animal you find.**

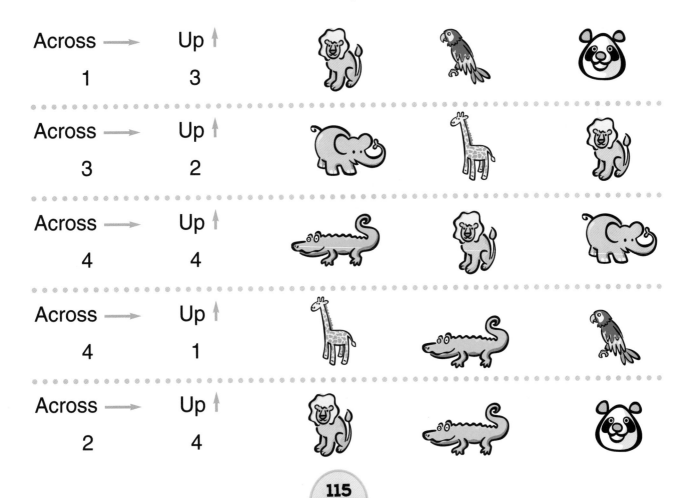

# Measuring Inches
Write the length of each object.

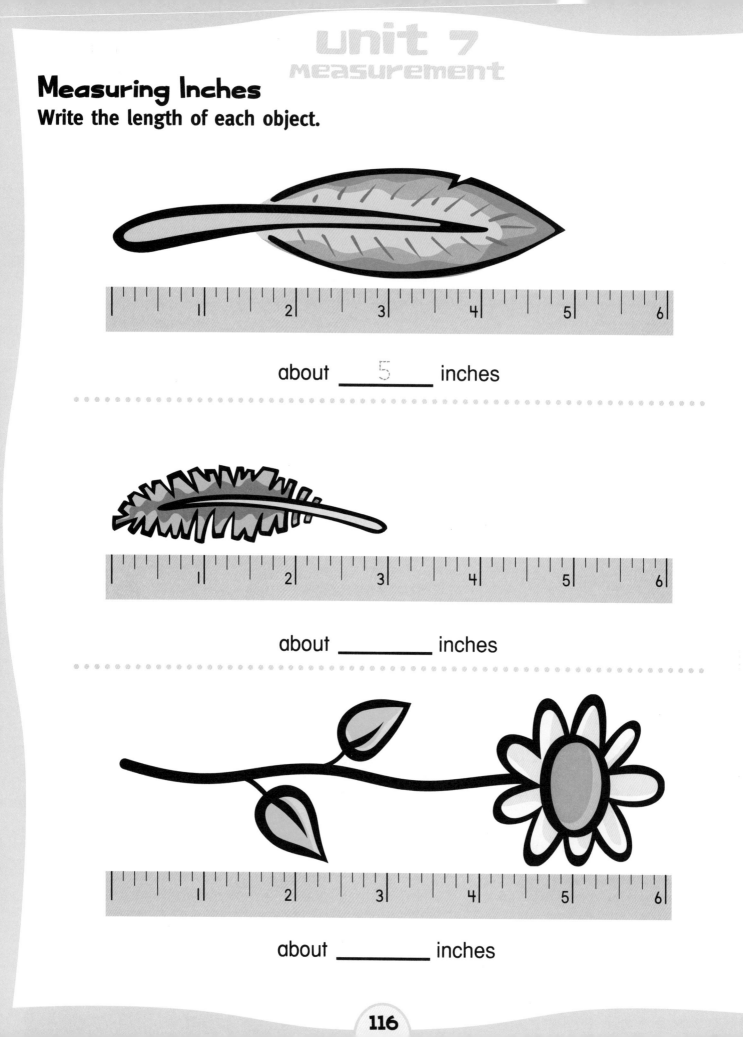

about ___5___ inches

about _____ inches

about _____ inches

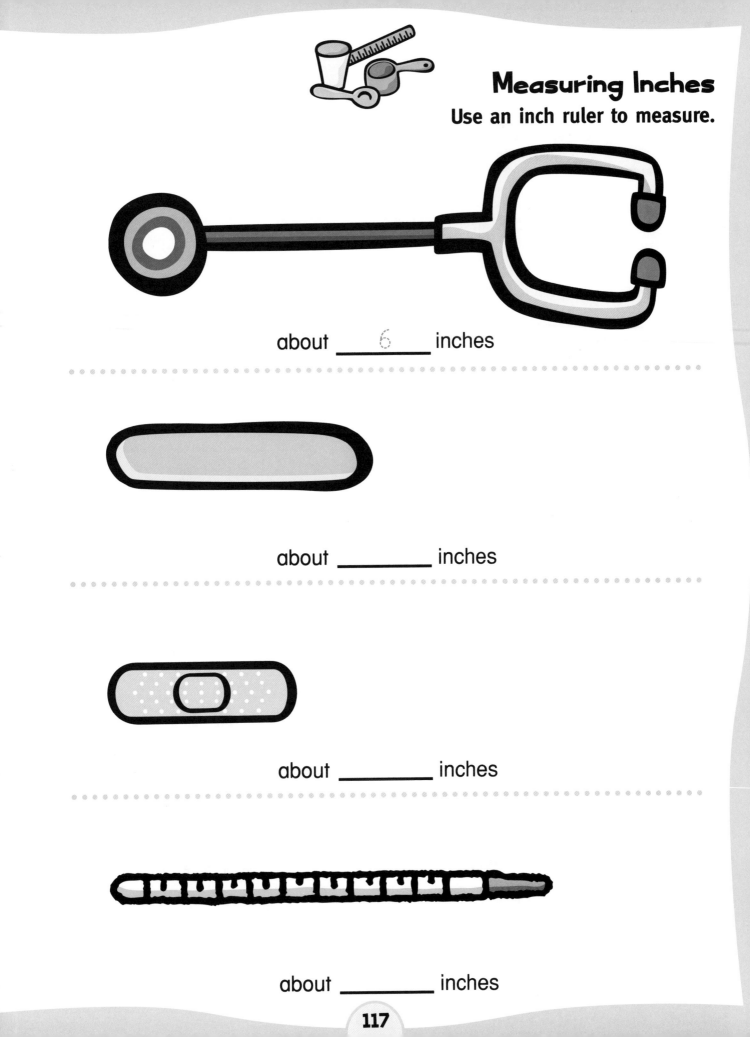

## Measuring Inches
### Use an inch ruler to measure.

about _____6_____ inches

about _____ inches

about _____ inches

about _____ inches

# Measuring Centimeters

**Write the length of each object.**

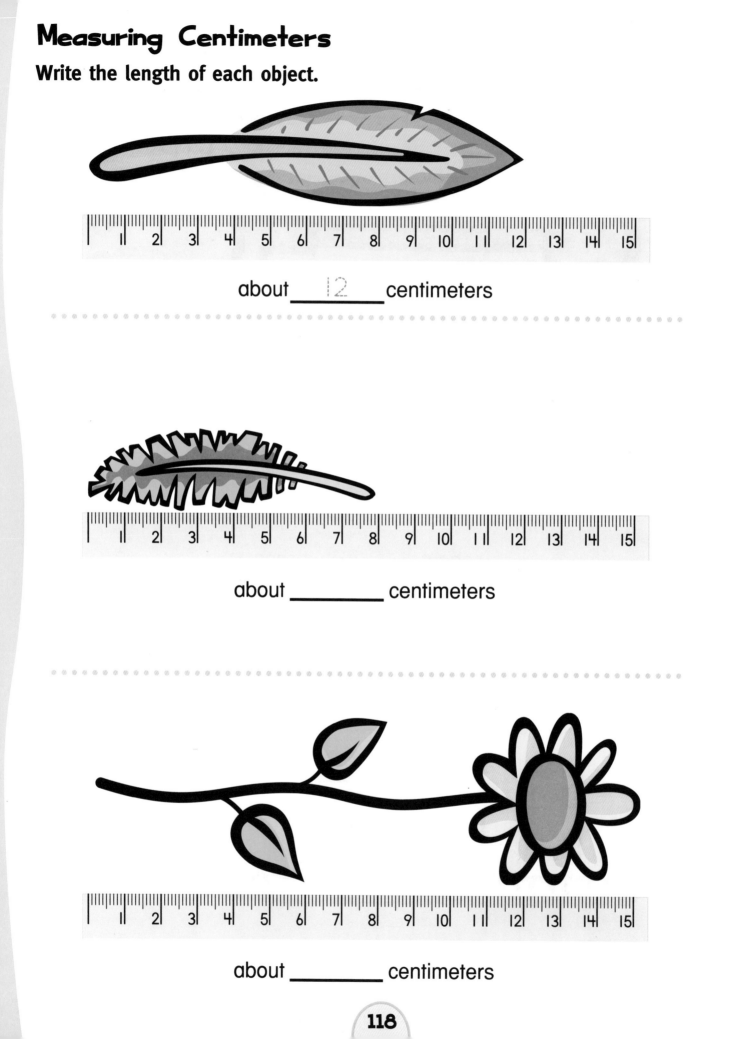

about _____12_____ centimeters

about _____ centimeters

about _____ centimeters

## Use a centimeter ruler to measure.

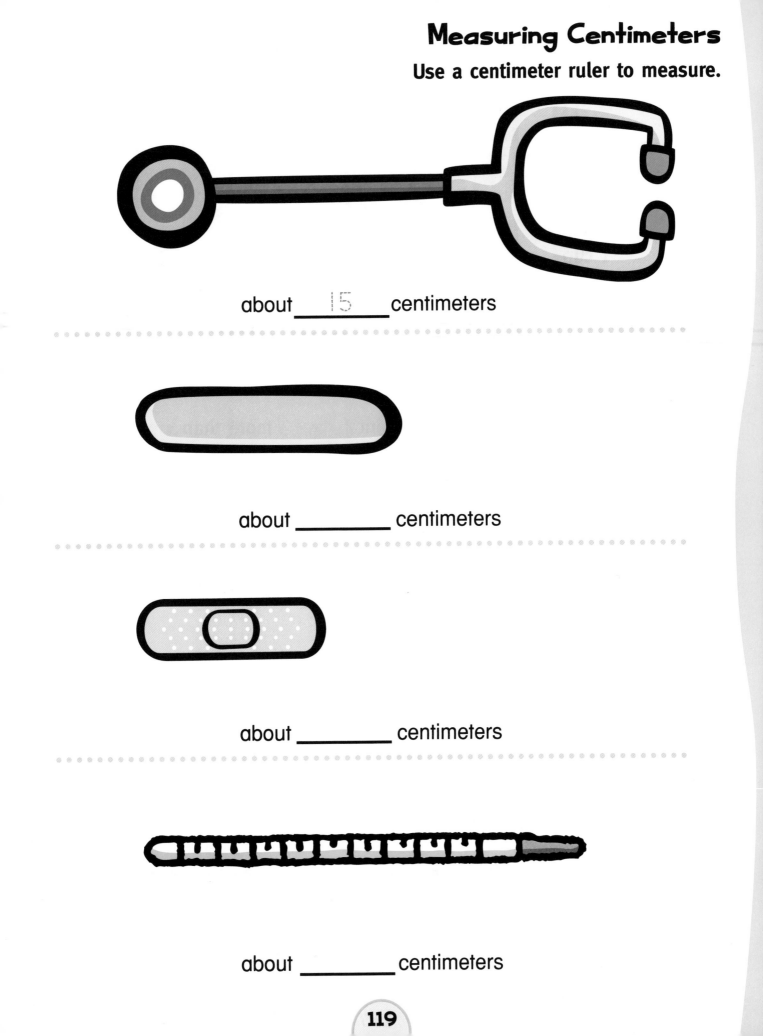

about \_\_\_\_15\_\_\_\_ centimeters

about _____ centimeters

about _____ centimeters

about _____ centimeters

# Cups, Pints, and Quarts

1 cup

1 pint

1 quart

**Circle how much each object can hold.**

   less than 1 pint   (more than 1 pint)

less than 1 quart   more than 1 quart

   less than 1 cup   more than 1 cup

   less than 1 quart   more than 1 quart

# Cups, Pints, and Quarts

1 pint fills 2 cups.

1 quart fills     2 pints     or     4 cups.

Circle how much each object can fill.

# Guess and Check

**Guess the length. Then measure to check.**

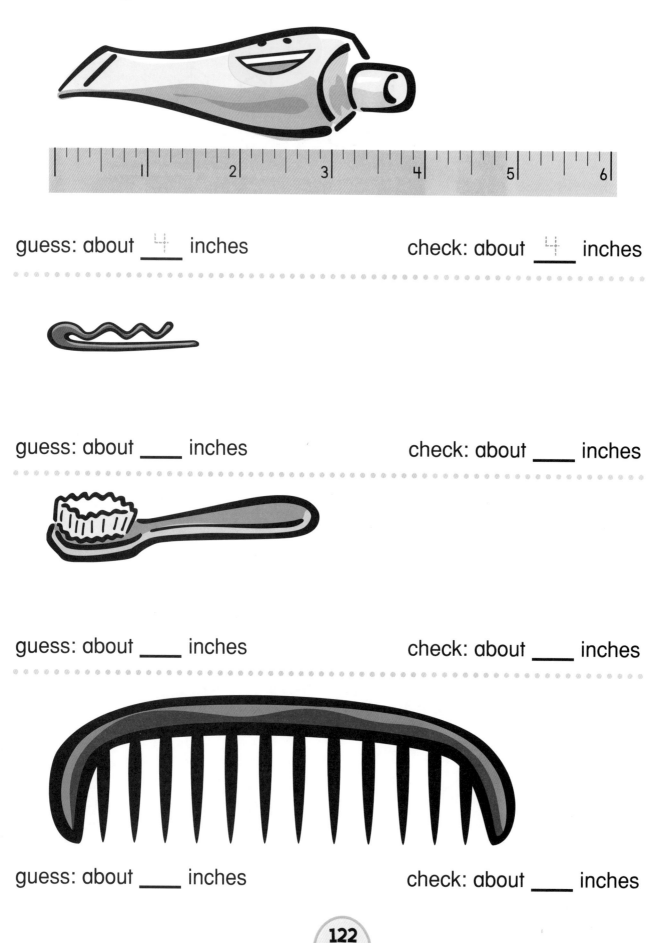

guess: about __4__ inches            check: about __4__ inches

guess: about ____ inches            check: about ____ inches

guess: about ____ inches            check: about ____ inches

guess: about ____ inches            check: about ____ inches

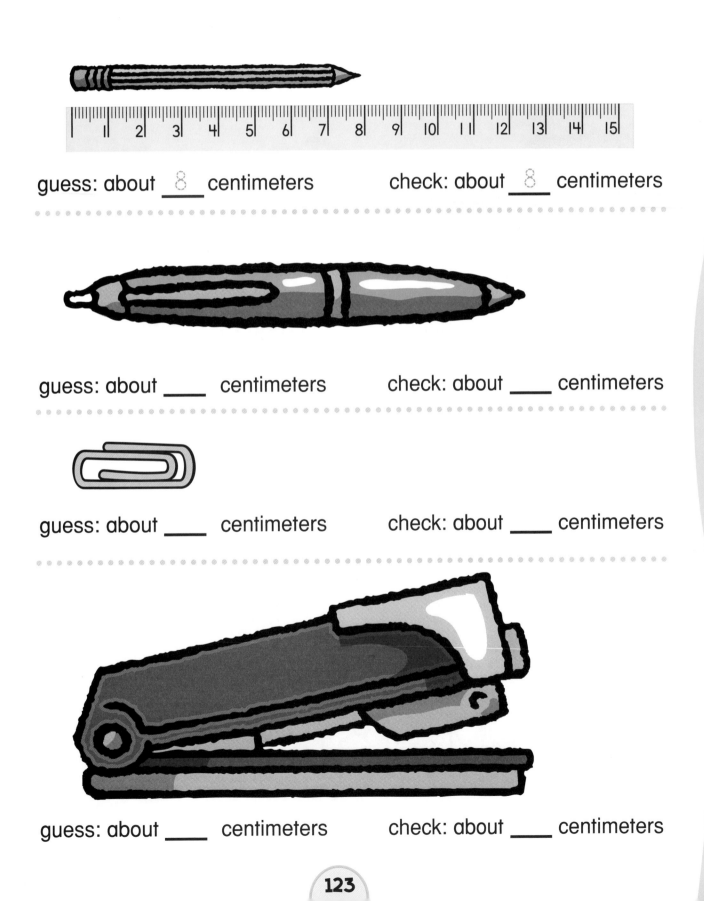

guess: about __8__ centimeters          check: about __8__ centimeters

guess: about ____ centimeters          check: about ____ centimeters

guess: about ____ centimeters          check: about ____ centimeters

guess: about ____ centimeters          check: about ____ centimeters

**Measure the lengths.**

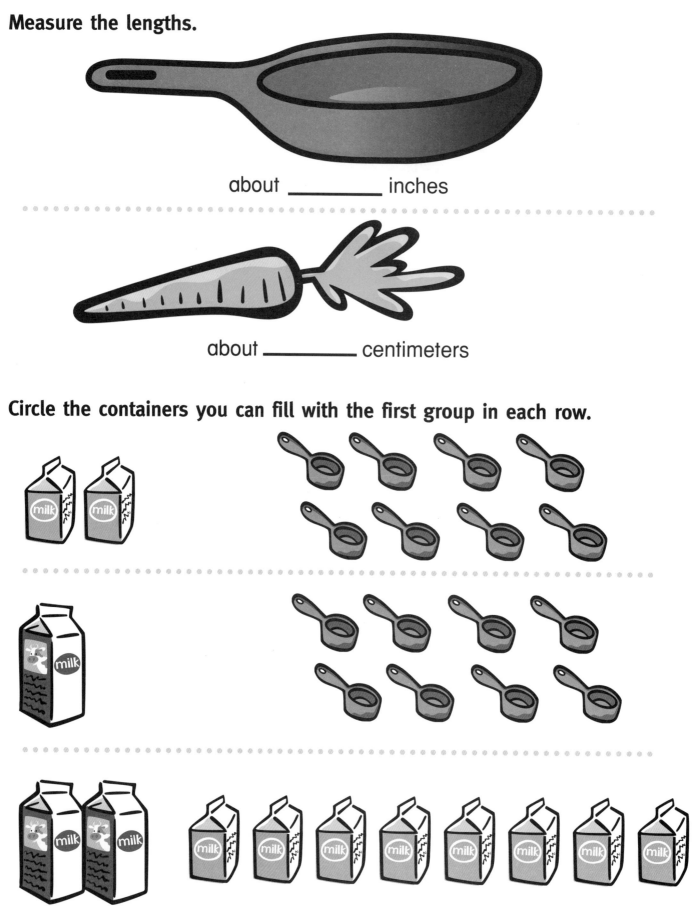

about _____ inches

about _____ centimeters

**Circle the containers you can fill with the first group in each row.**

**Guess the length. Then measure to check.**

guess: about ____ inches          check: about ____ inches

guess: about ____ inches          check: about ____ inches

guess: about ____ centimeters      check: about ____ centimeters

# Answer Key

## Page 6
Students should draw lines between numbers and the groups of flowers.
27 matches the third set of flowers.
44 matches the fourth set of flowers.
19 matches the first set of flowers.
35 matches the second set of flowers.

## Page 9
| | | | | |
|---|---|---|---|---|
| 17 | 18 | 19 | 20 | 21 |
| 64 | 65 | 66 | 67 | 68 |
| 96 | 97 | 98 | 99 | 100 |
| 38 | 39 | 40 | 41 | 42 |

## Page 10
15
21
42
53

## Page 11
| Tens | Ones | | | Tens | Ones | |
|---|---|---|---|---|---|---|
| 0 | 8 | = 8 | | 3 | 1 | = 31 |
| 6 | 6 | = 66 | | 4 | 9 | = 49 |
| 7 | 0 | = 70 | | 8 | 2 | = 82 |

## Page 12
| Hundreds | Tens | Ones |
|---|---|---|
| 2 | 3 | 6 |
| 3 | 1 | 4 |
| 2 | 4 | 8 |
| 3 | 2 | 0 |
| 1 | 8 | 4 |

## Page 13
| Hundreds | Tens | Ones | |
|---|---|---|---|
| 3 | 5 | 9 | = 359 |
| 5 | 1 | 3 | = 513 |
| 4 | 6 | 0 | = 460 |
| 2 | 9 | 8 | = 298 |

## Page 14
| | | | | |
|---|---|---|---|---|
| 139 | 140 | 141 | 142 | 143 |
| 98 | 99 | 100 | 101 | 102 |
| 116 | 117 | 118 | 119 | 120 |
| 146 | 147 | 148 | 149 | 150 |

## Page 16
136 matches the second model.
18 matches the third model.
205 matches the fourth model.
452 matches the first model.

## Page 17
14 < 16   19 > 2
33 < 57   28 > 25
40 > 39   36 > 26

## Page 18
| | |
|---|---|
| 43 | 30 |
| 89 | 147 |
| 176 | 30 |
| 13 | 71 |
| 10 | 114 |

## Page 19
seventh; 7th   fourth; 4th
first; 1st   ninth; 9th
third; 3rd   tenth; 10th
fifth; 5th   second; 2nd
sixth; 6th   eighth; 8th

## Page 20
thirteenth; 13th   seventeenth; 17th
eleventh; 11th   twentieth; 20th
twelfth; 12th   eighteenth; 18th
sixteenth; 16th   nineteenth; 19th
fifteenth; 15th   fourteenth; 14th

## Page 21
| | | |
|---|---|---|
| 5 | 10 | 15 |
| 10 | 20 | 30 |

| 5¢ | 10¢ | 15¢ | 20¢ | 25¢ | 30¢ |
|---|---|---|---|---|---|
| 10¢ | 20¢ | 30¢ | 40¢ | 50¢ | 60¢ |
| 35 | 40 | 45 | 50 | 55 | 60 |
| 50 | 60 | 70 | 80 | 90 | 100 |

## Page 22
| 2 | 4 | 6 | | | |
|---|---|---|---|---|---|
| 10 | 12 | 14 | 16 | 18 | 20 |
| 8 | 10 | 12 | 14 | 16 | 18 |
| 66 | 68 | 70 | 72 | 74 | 76 |
| 34 | 36 | 38 | 40 | 42 | 44 |
| 100 | 102 | 104 | 106 | 108 | 110 |
| 20 | 22 | 24 | 26 | 28 | 30 |

## Page 23
odd   even
even   odd
odd   odd
even   even

## Page 24

## Page 25
| | | | | | |
|---|---|---|---|---|---|
| 15 | 20 | 25 | 30 | 35 | 40 |
| 132 | 134 | 136 | 138 | 140 | 142 |
| 18 | 19 | 18 | 19 | 18 | 19 |
| 60 | 70 | 80 | 90 | 100 | 110 |
| 16 | 18 | 20 | 22 | 24 | 26 |
| 295 | 296 | 297 | 298 | 299 | 300 |
| 23 | 33 | 43 | 53 | 63 | 73 |
| 40 | 42 | 44 | 46 | 48 | 50 |

## Page 26
| | | | | | | | |
|---|---|---|---|---|---|---|---|
| 36 | 37 | 38 | 39 | 40 | 41 | 42 | 43 |
| 71 | 72 | 73 | 74 | 75 | 76 | 77 | 78 |
| 113 | 114 | 115 | 116 | 117 | 118 | 119 | 120 |
| 185 | 186 | 187 | 188 | 189 | 190 | 191 | 192 |

47 > 43   28 < 29
92   150
odd   even

## Page 27
65 matches the second model.
123 matches the third model.
48 matches the first model.

| | | | | | |
|---|---|---|---|---|---|
| 6 | 8 | 10 | 12 | 14 | 16 |
| 25 | 30 | 35 | 40 | 45 | 50 |
| 60 | 70 | 80 | 90 | 100 | 110 |
| 116 | 118 | 120 | 122 | 124 | 126 |

## Page 28
9
7
5
10

## Page 29
4 + 5 = 9
7 + 1 = 8
3 + 4 = 7
3 + 2 = 5
1 + 9 = 10

126

**Page 30**
13
11
15
18

**Page 31**
9 + 8 = 17
7 + 9 = 16
7 + 5 = 12
6 + 7 = 13
5 + 9 = 14

**Page 32**
| 1 + 0 = 1 | 0 + 2 = 2 |
| 3 + 0 = 3 | 0 + 4 = 4 |
| 5 + 0 = 5 | 0 + 6 = 6 |
| 7 + 0 = 7 | 0 + 8 = 8 |
| 9 + 0 = 9 | 10 + 0 = 10 |

**Page 33**
2 + 2 = 4
5 + 5 = 10
9 + 9 = 18
4 + 4 = 8
7 + 7 = 14

**Page 34**
| 9 | 9 |
| 10 | 10 |
| 7 | 7 |
| 8 | 8 |

**Page 35**
| 3 + 6 = 9 | 6 + 0 = 6 |
| 1 + 9 = 10 | 5 + 5 = 10 |
| 2 + 4 = 6 | 3 + 2 = 5 |

**Page 36**
27
38
59
48

**Page 37**
37
59
92
79

**Page 38**
| 87 | 79 | 23 | 57 |
| 56 | 85 | 99 | 54 |
| 92 | 93 | 38 | 94 |
| 89 | 79 | 48 | 89 |

**Page 39**
| 39 | 67 | 54 | 67 |
| 69 | 78 | 94 | 96 |
| 57 | 28 | 66 | 78 |
| 69 | 58 | 28 | 89 |
| 98 | 59 | 89 | 76 |
| 19 | 78 | 85 | 79 |

**Page 40**
Shading will show a rocket.

**Page 41**
356
279
428
597

**Page 42**
| 568 | 856 | 759 | 957 |
| 971 | 478 | 363 | 999 |
| 812 | 852 | 915 | 616 |

**Page 43**
0 tens 12 ones = 1 ten 2 ones = 12
2 tens 14 ones = 3 tens 4 ones = 34
1 ten 16 ones = 2 tens 6 ones = 26
4 tens 13 ones = 5 tens 3 ones = 53

**Page 44**
1 ten 13 ones = 23
2 tens 11 ones = 31
4 tens 10 ones = 50

**Page 45**
| 65 | 50 | 82 | 80 |
| 41 | 91 | 50 | 33 |
| 80 | 72 | 91 | 98 |

**Page 46**
| 63 | 66 | 80 | 42 |
| 71 | 65 | 50 | 75 |
| 84 | 70 | 90 | 25 |
| 81 | 31 | 62 | 30 |

**Page 47**
| 83 | 72 | 20 | 73 | 64 |
| 66 | 91 | 54 | 60 | 65 |
| 52 | 30 | 94 | 90 | 75 |
| 71 | 82 | 83 | 41 | 90 |

**Page 48**
| 71 | 82 | 51 | 80 | 73 |
| 72 | 82 | 72 | 53 | 72 |
| 72 | 41 | 72 | 42 | 62 |
| 72 | 72 | 72 | 43 | 72 |
| 72 | 61 | 72 | 81 | 72 |
| 72 | 82 | 72 | 82 | 72 |
Shading will show the word **Hi**.

**Page 49**
| 10 + 30 = 40 | 60 + 20 = 80 |
| 40 + 10 = 50 | 10 + 50 = 60 |
| 20 + 30 = 50 | 50 + 30 = 80 |
| 10 + 10 = 20 | |

**Page 50**
| 8 | 9 |
| 16 | 14 |
| 10 | 18 |
| 16 | 12 |
| 19 | 66 | 94 | 69 |
| 39 | 58 | 58 | 97 |
| 566 | 661 | 937 | 499 |
| 21 | 73 | 47 | 61 |
| 75 | 58 | 94 | 83 |

**Page 51**
| 4 + 19 = 23 | 5 + 23 = 28 |
| 2 + 48 = 50 | 3 + 71 = 74 |
| 40 + 20 = 60 | 30 + 50 = 80 |

**Page 52**
7
5
9
3
8

**Page 53**
4
1
6
2

**Page 54**
13
17
11
10
16

**Page 55**
12
9
14
11
15

**Page 56**
9 − 9 = 0
12 − 12 = 0
5 − 5 = 0
17 − 17 = 0
10 − 10 = 0

**Page 57**
11 − 0 = 11
18 − 0 = 18
3 − 0 = 3
5 − 0 = 5
14 − 0 = 14

**Page 58**
| 5 − 2 = 3 | 5 − 3 = 2 |
| 9 − 7 = 2 | 9 − 2 = 7 |
| 3 − 1 = 2 | 3 − 2 = 1 |
| 10 − 4 = 6 | 10 − 6 = 4 |

**Page 59**
| 6 + 2 = 8 | 5 + 3 = 8 |
| 2 + 6 = 8 | 3 + 5 = 8 |
| 8 − 6 = 2 | 8 − 5 = 3 |
| 8 − 2 = 6 | 8 − 3 = 5 |
| | |
| 5 + 4 = 9 | 6 + 3 = 9 |
| 4 + 5 = 9 | 3 + 6 = 9 |
| 9 − 5 = 4 | 9 − 6 = 3 |
| 9 − 4 = 5 | 9 − 3 = 6 |

**Page 60**
9 − 2 = 7
3 + 5 = 8
14 − 10 = 4
7 − 6 = 1
2 + 8 = 10

**Page 61**
4 + 3 = 7
12 − 4 = 8
6 + 3 = 9
11 − 6 = 5
13 − 9 = 4

**Page 62**
21
34
51
43
83

**Page 63**
15
22
23
17
21

**Page 64**
12
22
41
31
22

**Page 65**
| 71 | 15 | 32 | 1 |
| 53 | 17 | 20 | 44 |
| 23 | 11 | 43 | 10 |
| 31 | 33 | 99 | 12 |

**Page 66**
| 32 | 4 | 0 | 3 |
| 49 | 72 | 32 | 12 |
| 64 | 1 | 30 | 29 |
| 64 | 18 | 0 | 80 |
| 52 | 29 | 81 | 32 |
| 13 | 18 | 63 | 30 |

**Page 67**
Shading will show a house.

**Page 68**
| 412 | 209 | 641 | 510 |
| 714 | 180 | 999 | 223 |
| 510 | 392 | 347 | 510 |
| 933 | 886 | 437 | 132 |

**Page 69**
2 tens 3 ones = 1 ten 13 ones; 15
4 tens 1 one = 3 tens 11 ones; 35
3 tens 6 ones = 2 tens 16 ones; 27
5 tens 0 ones = 4 tens 10 ones; 43

**Page 70**
3 tens 5 ones = 2 tens 15 ones; 18
2 tens 1 one = 1 ten 11 ones; 7
4 tens 3 ones = 3 tens 13 ones; 14
6 tens 0 ones = 5 tens 10 ones; 23

**Page 71**
| 39 | 13 | 58 | 19 |
| 25 | 26 | 3 | 67 |
| 4 | 5 | 39 | 6 |

**Page 72**
| 26 | 18 | 37 | 25 |
| 44 | 47 | 47 | 48 |
| 37 | 38 | 15 | 68 |
| 17 | 26 | 4 | 39 |
| 49 | 5 | 38 | 15 |

**Page 73**
| 12 | 54 | 43 | 43 |
| 8 | 8 | 51 | 17 |
| 54 | 12 | 17 | 51 |
| 65 | 19 | 4 | 16 |
| 19 | 65 | 66 | 4 |
| 7 | 7 | 16 | 66 |

**Page 74**

| | | | |
|---|---|---|---|
| 29 | 75 | 18 | 29 |
| 86 | 3 | 2 | 43 |
| 38 | 37 | 9 | 13 |
| 9 | 78 | 31 | 19 |
| 19 | 6 | 8 | 59 |
| 17 | 19 | 13 | 9 |

**Page 75**

8 + 4 = 12
10 − 3 = 7
6 + 4 = 10
9 + 2 = 11
12 − 9 = 3

**Page 76**

| | |
|---|---|
| 0 | 9 |
| 6 | 8 |

5 + 4 = 9
4 + 5 = 9
9 − 5 = 4
9 − 4 = 5

7 + 3 = 10
3 + 7 = 10
10 − 7 = 3
10 − 3 = 7

| | | | |
|---|---|---|---|
| 15 | 22 | 13 | 27 |
| 330 | 431 | 334 | 71 |
| 9 | 6 | 8 | 5 |
| 29 | 34 | | |

**Page 77**

9 + 3 = 12
14 − 7 = 7
8 − 3 = 5
5 + 5 = 10

**Page 78 | Page 79 | Page 80**

| Page 78 | Page 79 | Page 80 |
|---|---|---|
| 5¢ | 8¢ | 16¢ |
| 12¢ | 10¢ | 15¢ |
| 17¢ | 13¢ | 20¢ |
| 15¢ | 15¢ | 24¢ |
| | 17¢ | 27¢ |

**Page 81 | Page 82**

| Page 81 | | Page 82 |
|---|---|---|
| 13¢ | 17¢ | 41¢ |
| 26¢ | 31¢ | 35¢ |
| 48¢ | 45¢ | 50¢ |
| | | 59¢ |
| | | 96¢ |

**Page 83**

32¢ matches the second set of coins.
56¢ matches the third set of coins.
65¢ matches the first set of coins.
45¢ matches the fourth set of coins.
28¢ matches the last set of coins.
70¢ matches the fifth set of coins.

**Page 84**

Possible answers are given.
1 dime, 1 nickel, 4 pennies
or 3 nickels, 4 pennies

1 quarter, 3 pennies
or 2 dimes, 1 nickel, 3 pennies

2 quarters, 1 dime, 2 pennies
or 6 dimes, 2 pennies

2 quarters, 4 dimes, 1 nickel,
2 pennies or 9 dimes, 1 nickel,
2 pennies

**Page 85**

Students should draw lines between
equal amounts of money.
1 nickel matches 5 pennies.
1 dime matches 2 nickels.
1 quarter matches 2 dimes and 1
nickel.
1 nickel and 2 pennies match 7
pennies.
2 quarters match 5 dimes.
1 quarter and 1 dime match 3 dimes
and 1 nickel.

**Page 86**

1 nickel or 5 pennies
1 dime or 2 nickels
  or 10 pennies
1 quarter or 5 nickels or 25 pennies
5 dimes or 10 nickels or 50 pennies
4 quarters or 10 dimes or
  100 pennies

**Page 87**

Students should circle the coins.
Possible answers are given.
35¢: Circle 1 quarter and 1 dime.
49¢: Circle 1 quarter, 2 dimes, and
  4 pennies.
17¢: Circle 1 dime, 1 nickel, and
  2 pennies.
89¢: Circle 3 quarters, 1 dime, and
  4 pennies.

**Page 88**

60¢; 2 quarters, 1 dime
50¢; 2 quarters
75¢; 3 quarters
65¢; 2 quarters, 1 dime, 1 nickel

**Page 89**

3¢
10¢
20¢
15¢

**Page 90 | Page 91 | Page 92**

| Page 90 | Page 91 | Page 92 |
|---|---|---|
| 20¢ | 22¢ | 15¢ |
| 3¢ | 5¢ | 21¢ |
| 2¢ | 10¢ | 20¢ |
| 8¢ | | |

**Page 92**

28¢
67¢
1 nickel or 5 pennies
1 dime or 2 nickels or 10 pennies
50¢; Students should draw 2 quarters.

**Page 93**

Possible answers are given.
1 dime, 1 nickel, 1 penny
or 1 dime, 6 pennies

2 quarters, 1 dime, 1 nickel
or 6 dimes, 1 nickel

4¢
8¢

**Page 94**

| | | |
|---|---|---|
| 4:00; 4 | 10:00; 10 | 6:00; 6 |
| 3:00; 3 | 8:00; 8 | 5:00; 5 |
| 7:00; 7 | 12:00; 12 | 2:00; 2 |

**Page 95**

| | | |
|---|---|---|
| 9:30 | 3:30 | 11:30 |
| 7:30 | 10:30 | 1:30 |
| 2:30 | 8:30 | 6:30 |
| 4:30 | 12:30 | 5:30 |

**Page 96**

| | | |
|---|---|---|
| 2:15 | 8:45 | 1:45 |
| 5:15 | 7:45 | 11:15 |
| 12:45 | 6:15 | 4:15 |
| 9:45 | 10:15 | 3:45 |

**Page 97**

| | |
|---|---|
| 7:15 | 11:45 |
| 1:45 | 8:15 |
| 3:15 | 10:45 |
| 5:45 | 9:15 |

**Page 98**

Clocks should show
the following times:
7:00
9:00
6:15
8:00

**Page 99**

10:05; 5 minutes after 10
1:25; 25 minutes after 1
7:55; 55 minutes after 7

10:15; 15 minutes after 10
9:40; 40 minutes after 9
11:10; 10 minutes after 11

**Page 100**

| | |
|---|---|
| 6:30 | 12:40 |
| 5:15 | 9:05 |
| 2:20 | 11:50 |
| 1:35 | 8:00 |

**Page 101**

5:45 matches the third clock.
2:30 matches the fourth clock.
12:05 matches the last clock.
9:15 matches the first clock.
3:10 matches the second clock.

**Page 103**

2nd; 1st; 3rd
2nd; 3rd; 1st
2nd; 3rd; 1st
2nd; 1st; 3rd

**Page 104**

| | | |
|---|---|---|
| 5:00 | 9:00 | 12:00 |
| 10:30 | 2:30 | 7:30 |
| 3:15 | 8:45 | 11:15 |
| 2:25 | 6:40 | 10:05 |

**Page 105**

10:00
2:00
1:15
7:45

**Page 106**

cubes–die
pyramids–ancient pyramid
spheres–Earth
cones–traffic cone
cylinders–trash can

**Page 107**

triangle—warning sign
circle—bullseye
square—cd case
rectangle—beware sign

**Page 108**

square; 4
triangle; 3
rectangle; 4
circle; 0
rectangle; 4
triangle; 3
square; 4

**Page 111**

| | |
|---|---|
| 9 units | 4 units |
| 6 units | 3 units |
| 5 units | 12 units |

**Page 112**

Students should circle
each map location.
pizza parlor
city hall
downtown
home
school

**Page 113**

| Across | Up |
|---|---|
| 5 | 3 |
| 3 | 4 |
| 7 | 1 |
| 1 | 2 |

**Page 114**

squares
cones
spheres
rectangles
  9 units
  4 units

**Page 115**

parrot
elephant
lion
giraffe
panda

**Page 116**

5 in., 3 in., 6 in.

**Page 117**

6 in., 3 in., 2 in., 5 in.

**Page 118**

12 cm, 8 cm, 15 cm

**Page 119**

15 cm
7 cm
5 cm
13 cm

**Page 120**

more than 1 pint
less than 1 quart
less than 1 cup
more than 1 quart
more than 1 pint

**Page 121**

2 cups, 2 pints, 4 cups, 4 cups

**Page 122** Guesses may vary.
4 in., 2 in., 3 in., 5 in.

**Page 123** Guesses may vary.
8 cm, 13 cm, 3 cm, 14 cm

**Page 124**

5 in.
10 cm
4 cups
4 cups
4 pints

**Page 125** Guesses may vary.

1 in.
6 in.
7 cm